COMPLETE

Guitar for the Absolute Beginner

Absolutely everything you need to know to start playing now!

National Guitar Workshop Method

Approved Curriculum

Susan Mazer

Alfred, the leader in educational publishing, and the

National Guitar Workshop, one of America's finest guitar schools,

have joined forces to bring you the best,

most progressive educational tools possible.

We hope you will enjoy this book and encourage you to

look for other fine products from

Alfred and the National Guitar Workshop.

Acquisition, editorial: Nathaniel Gunod, Workshop Arts
Interior design: Cathy Bolduc, Workshop Arts
Music typesetting: Joe Bouchard, Workshop Arts
Author photos: Stuart Rabinowitz
Cover photos: Dry Lake Bed © Photodisc, Inc.; Hatching © West Stock, Inc.

D1260464

Alfred

Alfred Publishing Co., Inc.
16320 Roscoe Blvd., Suite 100
P.O. Box 10003
Van Nuys, CA 91410-0003
alfred.com

Copyright © MMVII by Alfred Publishing Co., Inc.
All rights reserved. Printed in USA.

Book and DVD (with case)
ISBN-10: 0-7390-4669-1
ISBN-13: 978-0-7390-4669-2

Book and DVD (without case)
ISBN-10: 0-7390-4670-5
ISBN-13: 978-0-7390-4670-8

Table of Contents

Table of Contents

About the Author

Philadelphia-born Susan Mazer now lives and works in Connecticut. She received her Bachelor of Music degree from the Hartt School of Music. Susan is on the faculty at The Hartford Conservatory, where she teaches theory and ear training. Since 1989, she has taught fingerstyle guitar at the National Guitar Summer Workshop. Susan has been performing for the last fifteen years with an acoustic duo. She is the host of the popular instructional video *Guitar for the Absolute Beginner* which parallels this series.

⦿ Acknowledgements

Thank you to all of my students, from whom I learn so much, the Smolovers and Nat Gunod, Paula Dutton, Jean Gray, The Music Shop, Jerry Schurr, Carol, Mindy and most of all, my mother, Judy.

⦿ Dedication

My father taught me how to love life and music. Music will always remind me of him.

DVD Audio Menu

About the DVD

The companion DVD contains all the audio tracks found in this book. To access these tracks, select **Audio Tracks** from the main menu.

Shopping for Your Guitar

Buying your first guitar does not have to be intimidating. You just need to know what to look for. Here are a few pointers to help make your first purchase a little easier.

1) Make a choice between buying an acoustic or an electric guitar.

Electric and the acoustic guitars are played in exactly the same way. It is a common misconception that it is best to start learning on an acoustic guitar. Make your purchase based on the style of music and the sound you like. If you decide to buy an acoustic guitar, you can choose between one of two basic types: classical or folk. The classical guitar has nylon strings, which give it a mellow sound appropriate for classical or soft music. The folk guitar has steel strings, which are slightly more difficult to play at first, but give it a louder, brighter sound appropriate for more popular styles of music. If the student is under nine or ten years old, a ¾ size classical guitar is a wise choice. If you decide to buy an electric guitar, you have a huge variety of brands, sizes and shapes to choose from.

2) Have a salesperson demonstrate the guitars for you.

Only you know the sound you like. Depending on the wood, the body size, the type of pickups (if it is electric) and the make of the guitar, the sound will vary drastically. You do not have to spend a lot of money to get a quality instrument. There are $250 guitars that sound better than some $650 guitars. Trust your ear.

3) Take into consideration the size of the guitar.

Both the size of the body and the neck (see page 7, Parts of the Guitar) vary slightly from instrument to instrument. Acoustic guitars range in size from the largest jumbo body to a standard dreadnaught size, down to a smaller folk size. Have a salesperson let you hold the guitar. Choose one that feels comfortable to you. If you are shopping for an electric guitar, you will find the body and neck sizes vary widely from brand to brand and style to style. For instance, a traditional jazz guitar will have a much bigger body than a guitar traditionally used for rock.

4) Buy a used guitar with caution.

Although buying a used guitar is less expensive, it is important that you know what to look for. Try to make your purchase from a music shop with either an exchange policy or a warranty. Have a teacher or a friend who plays look it over. Certain kinds of repairs will not be worth your investment.

Parts of the Guitar

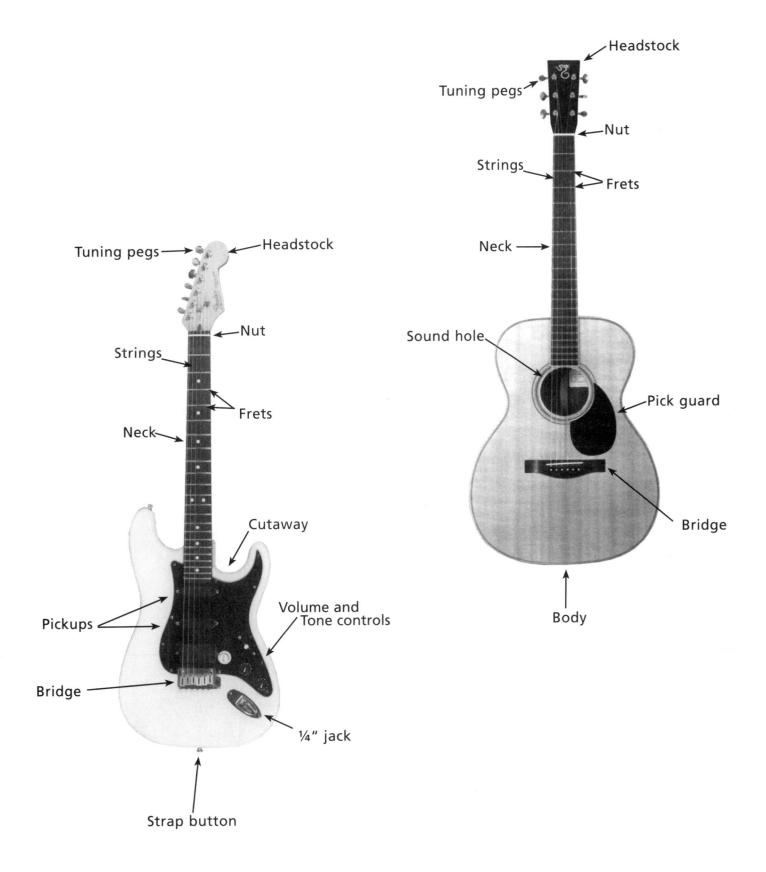

Tuning pegs

Headstock

Nut

Strings

Frets

Neck

Cutaway

Pickups

Volume and
Tone controls

Bridge

¼" jack

Strap button

Headstock

Tuning pegs

Nut

Strings

Frets

Neck

Sound hole

Pick guard

Bridge

Body

Holding the Guitar

The guitar should feel like an extension of your body. If you feel uncomfortable while you are playing, chances are that you are not holding the guitar properly.

The neck of the guitar should always be tilted upward. In this position, your arm has better access to the fingerboard, and your elbow will fall naturally at your side. Also, there is a minimum of tension in your shoulders, arms and hands, which results in easier playing and a better sound overall.

Three Positions for Playing the Guitar

A **Seated with a guitar strap.**

The strap will keep the neck in an upward position.

B **Seated with a footstool.**

The guitar sits on your left knee, which is elevated.

C **Standing with a strap.**

The strap holds the guitar in the proper playing position and allows you to move around freely (or dance around like your favorite rock star).

Left-Hand Technique

When playing the guitar, the left and right hands each have a specific job. The left hand will hold down the strings against the frets to play the melody (single notes that make up the main theme of the song), or the chords (a combination of notes that support the melody).

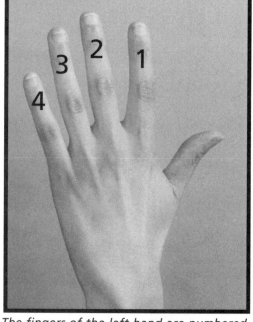

Before you begin to play, here are a few tips that will improve the quality of your playing:

The fingers of the left hand are numbered.

1) Your left thumb should stay straight on the back of the neck, behind the 2nd finger. The fingers will be pressing against strings, and the thumb will push back slightly from the other side.

2) Notes should be played on your fingertips. This keeps the fingers from leaning on any unwanted strings and creating extra sounds or preventing strings from ringing in a chord.

3) Your palm should be relaxed and away from the neck.

4) Fingers should be placed firmly behind (just to the left of) the fret, and not directly over the fret wire.

5) Fingernails on the left hand must be short so that they don't interfere with holding the strings securely against the frets.

Right-Hand Technique

The right hand has the job of strumming or picking the strings of the guitar. This will create the *rhythm* of the song. Rhythm is the organization of music in time—the arrangement of long and short notes.

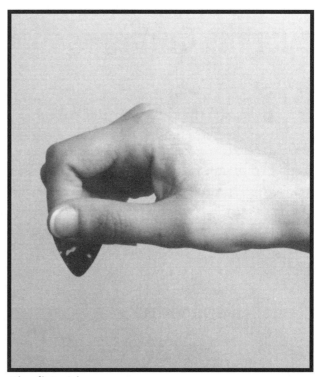

You may either choose to use your thumb alone or use a pick. If you decide to use a pick, sometimes called a *flat pick*, here's how to hold it:

Hold the pick firmly between the thumb and index finger.

The flat pick.

If the guitar is to be strummed downward, towards the floor, this symbol is used:

If the guitar is to be strummed upward, towards the ceiling, this symbol is used:

Another type of pick is called a *thumb pick*. It fits on your right-hand thumb and leaves your fingers free to pick or strum.

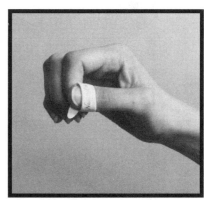

The type of pick you choose is a matter of preference. Picks come in varying degrees of thickness: heavy, medium and thin. There are literally hundreds of different styles and shapes of picks, so try several kinds and use what feels and sounds best to you.

The thumb pick.

Tuning the Guitar

Each time you pick up your guitar to play, you will need to make sure it is in tune. Playing out of tune is like driving with a flat tire. You won't get far.

Keep in mind that tuning is a skill that improves with practice because your ear will take time to develop. While you are learning, you are bound to break a few strings. Consider it your initiation into the world of guitar playing. Individual strings are inexpensive and are very easy to change.

String Names and Numbers

It is a good idea to begin by learning the names of the guitar strings. The thinnest string with the highest in pitch (highness or lowness) is the 1st string, high E. The next string is the 2nd string, B, then the 3rd string, G, 4th string, D, 5th string, A and the thickest string with the lowest pitch is the 6th string, low E.

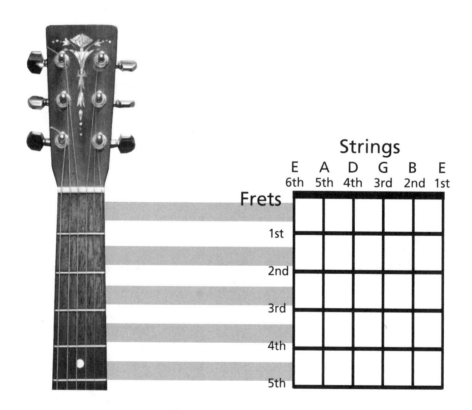

Methods for Tuning

The Piano

The six open strings of the guitar are the same notes as the six piano keys shown below. Compare the sound of each of your strings to those keys on the piano. If your note (a note is a musical sound) sounds too low, you need to tighten the string, raising the pitch. If your note sounds too high, you need to loosen the string, lowering the pitch. Change the pitch of each string by turning the tuning pegs.

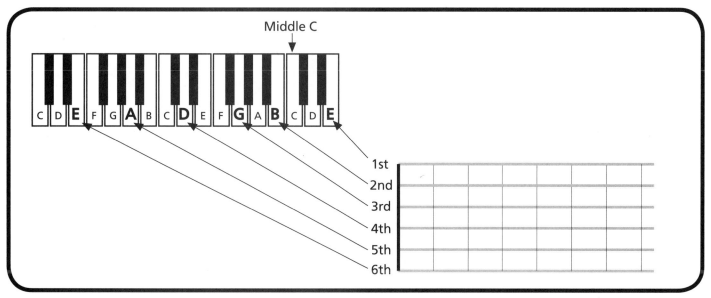

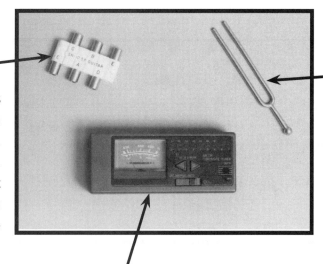

Pitch Pipe

A pitch pipe has six pipes that correspond to each of the open guitar strings. When you blow on a pipe, it will sound the correct pitch for its string. You then tune the string to the sound of that note.

The Tuning Fork

A tuning fork, when struck, will give you a reference pitch to tune to (see Relative Tuning, page 14). (Guitarists usually use an E tuning fork, although tuning forks in A are widely available.)

Electronic Tuners

An electronic tuner will automatically read a pitch and show you with a needle and LED lights when you are in tune. This may be the easiest method for beginners. The tuner will show you whether a note is high (sharp) or low (flat), which will help train your ear.

Relative Tuning

Relative tuning is the most common method of tuning the guitar. After getting a reference pitch, the guitar is then tuned to itself.

1) Tune the 6th string to E below middle C. If you have no piano, use a tuning fork, someone else's guitar, or somehow approximate E as best you can.

2) Press the 5th fret of the 6th string with your left hand. Tune the open 5th string to this pitch.

3) Press the 5th fret of the 5th string. Tune the open 4th string to this pitch.

4) Press the 5th fret of the 4th string. Tune the open 3rd string to this pitch.

5) Press the 4th fret of the 3rd string. Tune the open 2nd string to this pitch.

6) Press the 5th fret of the 2nd string. Tune the open 1st string to this pitch.

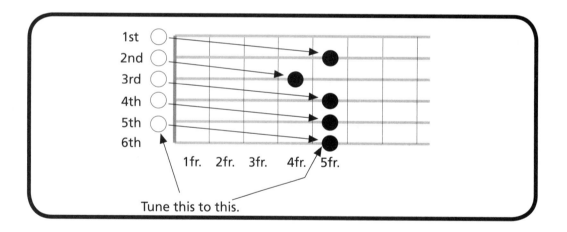

Tune this to this.

Using the companion DVD for this book, you can tune your guitar to the tuning notes on the first track.

Tuning

track 1

Your First Two Chords: G and D7

Chords are three or more notes played simultaneously. They have a much fuller sound than the individual strings we have been playing.

Chord diagrams, or chord boxes, show you how to play a chord. They display a picture of the guitar neck oriented vertically. The vertical lines are the guitar strings, and the horizontal lines are the frets. The string to the far left is the thickest, lowest string—the 6th, low E string. The black dots show you where to put your fingers. The numbers at the top of the box are the left hand fingers that play the notes. An "X" means that a string should not be played, and a "0" denotes an open string.

Let's take a look at two basic chords.

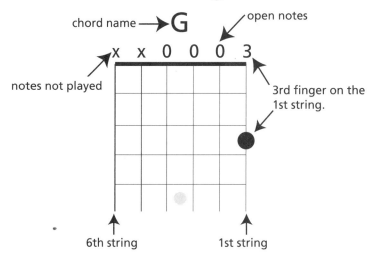

Chord Diagram

chord name → G   open notes

x   x   0   0   0   3

notes not played

3rd finger on the 1st string.

6th string   1st string

The G Chord

The 3rd finger plays the 1st string, 3rd fret. Strum the highest four strings. To strum, strike all the strings in the chord with one smooth downward (towards the floor) motion of your pick or thumb.

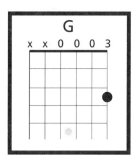

The D7 Chord

The 1st finger plays the 2nd string, 1st fret. The 2nd finger plays the 3rd string, 2nd fret. The 3rd finger plays the 1st string, 2nd fret. Strum down over the highest four strings.

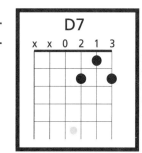

Chord Playing Tip
When changing from G to D7, simply slide the 3rd finger back a fret without lifting it off the fingerboard.

The first tune that you are going to play is in $\frac{4}{4}$, or *common time*. This is the time signature and it means that each *measure*, or grouping of notes, gets four *beats*. A beat is an equal division of time (like a heartbeat). Every measure with four beats is divided by a *bar line*. For now, we will use a single straight line as a time line for our music.

With your right hand thumb, or with your pick, strum down from the 4th to the 1st string, four times for each measure. Try to keep each beat equal.

Here are the chords you will need to play this tune:

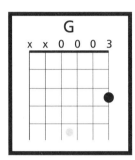

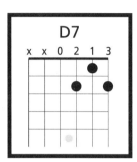

Learning to Fly

 track 2

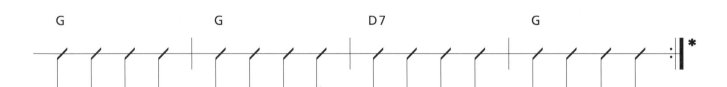

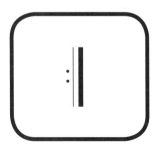

* This is the symbol for a repeat sign.

This will signal you to play the example or song a second time.

The C Chord

The next song uses a new chord. Let's take a look at it:

The C Chord

The 1st finger plays the 2nd string, 1st fret.
The 2nd finger plays the 4th string, 2nd fret.
Strum down over the highest four strings.

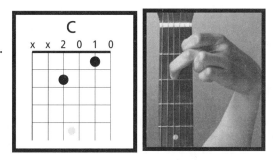

When changing from the C chord to the D7 chord, keep the lst finger down because it is a common tone between the two chords.

This song also has four beats per measure. This time, instead of strumming down on each beat, alternate down-stums and up-strums, strumming down-up-down-up. The chords in this tune use only the first four strings, so only strum over these strings.

Smooth Sailing

track 3

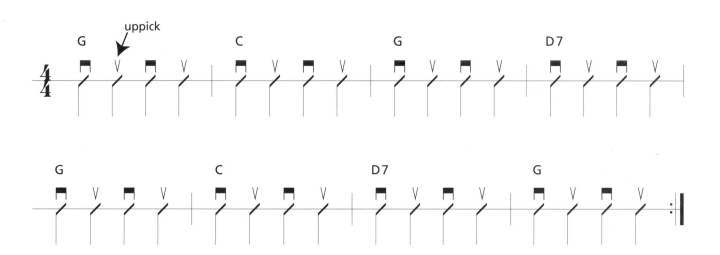

Reading Tablature

Tablature, or TAB, is a graphic way of notating guitar music. This is not the same as reading standard music notation. We will investigate that starting on page 26.

Tablature consists of six lines, each line representing a string of the guitar.

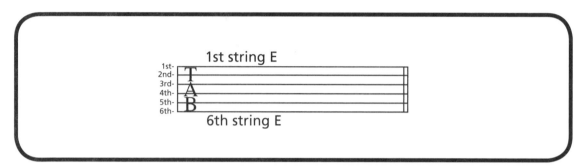

The numbers that are placed on the lines represent the frets to be played.

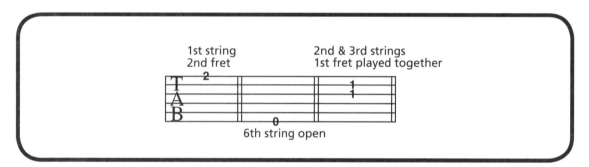

The numbers that are placed under the lines tell you which left hand finger to use.

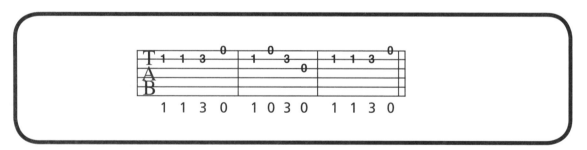

Worksheet #1 (answers on page 71)

1. Write the location of each note shown in the TAB, then play each note.

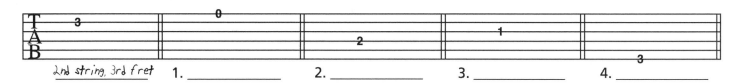

2nd string, 3rd fret   1. _____   2. _____   3. _____   4. _____

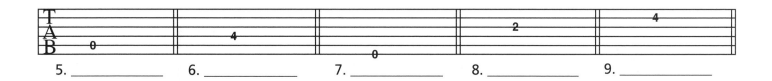

5. _____   6. _____   7. _____   8. _____   9. _____

2. The examples below are excerpts from well-known tunes. Using the TAB and dots (indicating short notes) and lines (indicating long notes), play through each and write down their names.

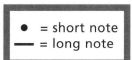

● = short note
— = long note

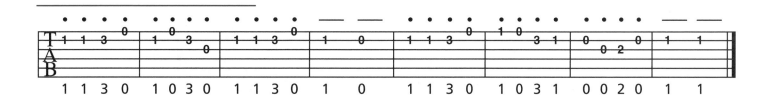

1 1 3 0   1 0 3 0   1 1 3 0   1 0   1 1 3 0   1 0 3 1   0 0 2 0   1   1

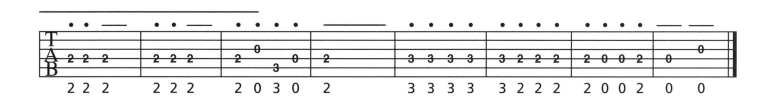

2 2 2   2 2 2   2 0 3 0   2   3 3 3 3   3 2 2 2   2 0 0 2   0   0

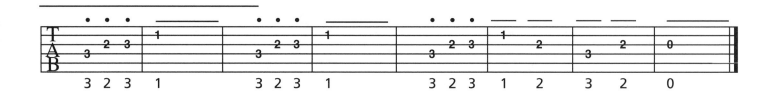

3 2 3   1   3 2 3   1   3 2 3   1   2   3   2   0

Three More Chords: A, D and E

There are literally thousands of songs that you can play with these three chords alone! There is a list of some of them page 70.

The A Chord
The 1st finger plays the 4th string, 2nd fret.
The 2nd finger plays the 3rd string, 2nd fret.
The 3rd finger plays the 2nd string, 2nd fret.
Strum down over the top five strings.

It will help to rotate your hand out slightly, so that you can get all three fingers as close to the fret as possible. The 1st finger will not get as close as the 3rd finger.

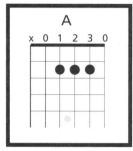

The D Chord
The 1st finger plays the 3rd string, 2nd fret.
The 2nd finger plays the 1st string, 2nd fret.
The 3rd finger plays the 2nd string, 3rd fret.
Strum down over the top four strings.

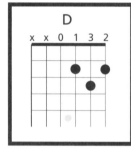

The E Chord
The 1st finger plays the 3rd string, 1st fret.
The 2nd finger plays the 5th string, 2nd fret.
The 3rd finger plays the 4th string, 2nd fret.
Strum down over all six strings.

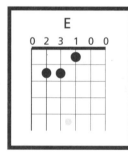

Chord Playing Tip
- When switching from the A to the E chord, the 2nd and 3rd fingers move together from the 3rd and 2nd strings to the 5th and 4th strings.

- When switching from the E to the D chord, the 1st finger stays on the 3rd string and moves from the 1st to the 2nd fret.

- Do not get frustrated if the transitions between the A,D and E chords are slow. Your muscles have a memory and the more times you play these progressions, the faster you will be able to change between them. This is the way every great guitar player got started.

This eight-bar ("bar" is another word for "measure") tune will help you practice the new chords that you have learned. Strum down four times in each measure.

Goin' to the Country

track 4

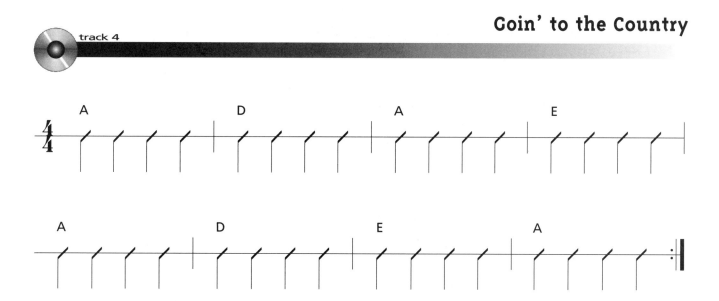

Bass Strum

A common method of chord strumming is to single out the *bass* note, and then strum the rest of the chord. The bass is the lowest sounding note in the chord. For instance, when you strum the five strings of the A chord, the 5th string, A, is the bass note. Here are the bass notes for the three chords in *Goin' to the Country*.

E chord = 6th string, low E
A chord = 5th string, A
D chord = 4th string, D

In each measure, pluck the bass note, then strum down over the highest three, four or five strings. This pattern happens twice per measure.

Goin' to the Country Bass Strum

track 5

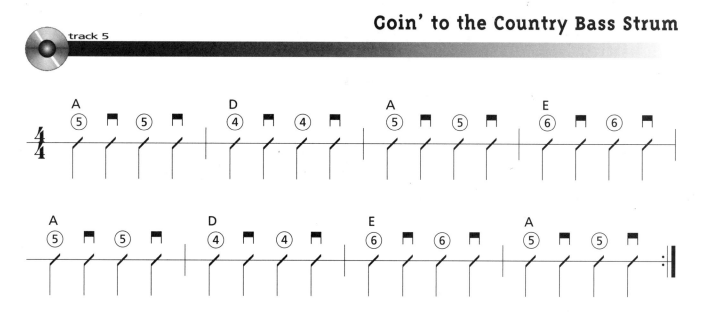

Fingerstyle

So far, your right hand has been strumming the strings. An alternative to strumming is *fingerstyle*, or *fingerpicking*. Instead of the notes in a chord being played all at once, they are played individually, or *arpeggiated*. A chord that is played in this manner is called an *arpeggio*.

Each finger on the right hand has a string that it almost always plays:

p ⟵ **Thumb.** Plays the bass strings: 6th, 5th and 4th.
i ⟵ **Index finger.** Plays the 3rd string.
m ⟵ **Middle finger.** Plays the 2nd string.
a ⟵ **Ring finger.** Plays the 1st string.

To strike the strings with the fingers (*i*, *m* and *a*), pull them inward towards the palm. The hand should be still and not pull away from the strings. To play the bass notes with *p*, move the whole thumb as one unit across the string towards the *i* finger.

Below are two fingerpicking patterns to try. The diagrams should be read left to right, and show which string to play, and with which finger. Count "1, 2, 3, 4" evenly and play the indicated string on each beat.

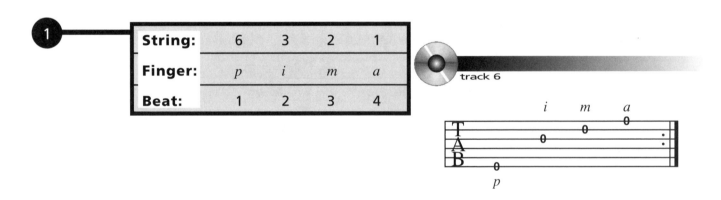

1

String:	6	3	2	1
Finger:	*p*	*i*	*m*	*a*
Beat:	1	2	3	4

track 6

In this one, *i*, *m* and *a* play simultaneously.

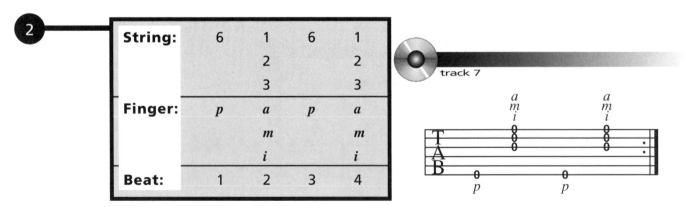

2

String:	6	1	6	1
		2		2
		3		3
Finger:	*p*	*a*	*p*	*a*
		m		*m*
		i		*i*
Beat:	1	2	3	4

track 7

This song is played fingerstyle. Use *p*, *i*, *m* and *a* of the right hand to strike the strings. Play the notes evenly, in groups of four.

A Long Winter

track 8

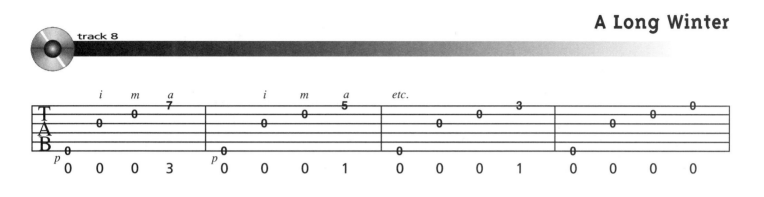

In this tune, your thumb (*p*) plays the bass notes, then *i*, *m* and *a* pluck the 3rd, 2nd and 1st strings simultaneously.

Single File

track 9

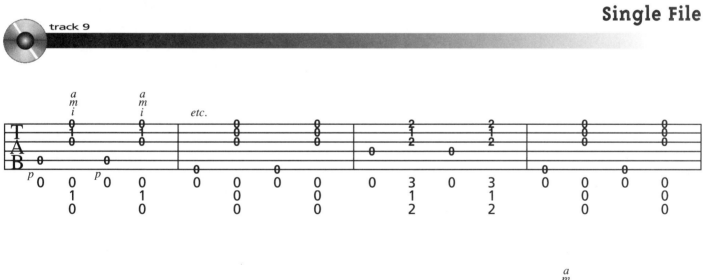

Three Minor Chords: Amin, Dmin and Emin

Minor chords are indicated with "min" next to the chord letter name. Unlike the major chords that we have learned, minor chords have a sad and solemn sound.

The Amin Chord
The 1st finger plays the 2nd string, 1st fret.
The 2nd finger plays the 4th string, 2nd fret.
The 3rd finger plays the 3rd string, 2nd fret.
Strum down over the top five strings.

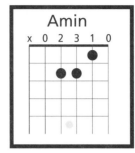

The Dmin Chord
The 1st finger plays the 1st string, 1st fret.
The 2nd finger plays the 3rd string, 2nd fret.
The 3rd finger plays the 2nd string, 3rd fret.
Strum down over the top four strings.

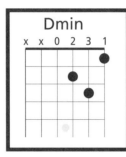

The Emin Chord
The 2nd finger plays the 5th string, 2nd fret.
The 3rd finger plays the 4th string, 2nd fret.
Strum down over all six strings.

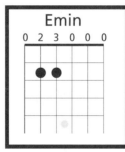
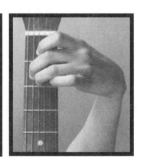

Chord Playing Tip
When moving from Amin to Emin, the 2nd and 3rd fingers will move as a pair from the 4th and 3rd strings to the 5th and 4th strings.

Try these minor chords with a bass/strum pattern.

Final Exam—Bass Strum

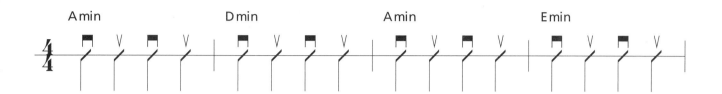

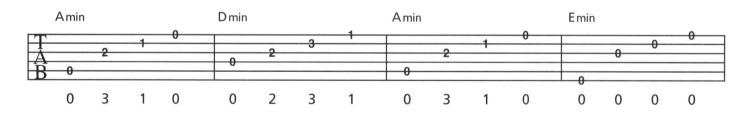

Let's apply fingerstyle technique to the minor chords.

Final Exam—Fingerstyle

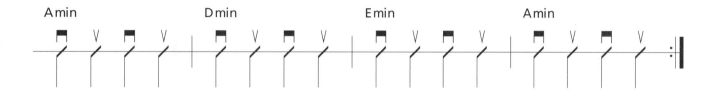

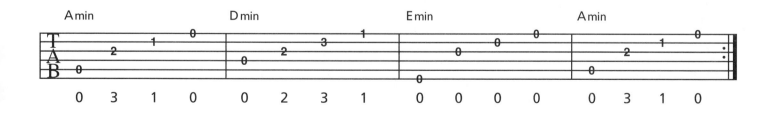

Reading Standard Music Notation

Learning to read music is surprisingly simple. Just a little music theory will tie all of the information in this book together.

Music has a seven-letter alphabet: A, B, C, D, E, F and G. Every note (musical sound) has one of these letter names. As you progress forward through the alphabet, the notes sound higher.   After G, the alphabet repeats itself. The A that comes after G is one *octave* higher than the first A. It is the same note, but higher in pitch (twelve frets).

Music is written on a *staff* consisting of five lines and four spaces. The location of a note on the staff tells you which note to play. You will find a G clef, or treble clef, at the beginning of every song. The tail of the G clef wraps around the G line to help you know the names of the notes on the staff. There are numerous clefs, but guitar music is always written in G clef.

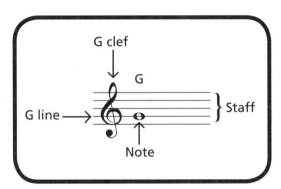

The notes on the lines are named as follows:

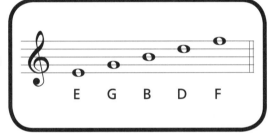

The notes in the spaces are named as follows:

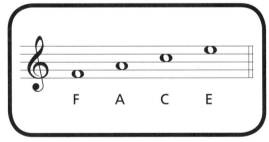

When we put the lines and spaces together, we create the whole musical alphabet:

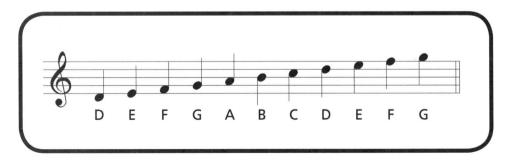

Worksheet #2 (answers on page 71)

Find the missing letters reading the notes on the staff. Then write the letters in the blanks.

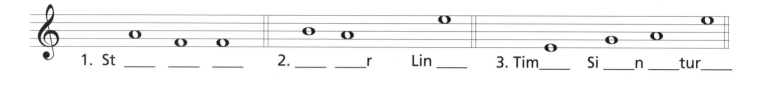

1. St ___ ___ ___   2. ___ ___r Lin ___   3. Tim___ Si ___n ___tur___

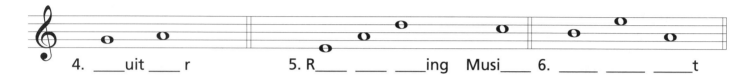

4. ___uit ___ r   5. R___ ___ ___ing Musi___   6. ___ ___ ___t

Musical Alphabet Puzzle

Circle all the words in the square that use only letters from the musical alphabet (there are twelve). Then write each word on the staff in music notes.

```
E   X  (B   E   D)  F   D   D   S   T   U
B   L   M   Z   Y   E   M   A   D   P   L
T   O   U   L   R   U   N   D   X   O   K
E   C   F   E   E   D   B   Q   M   P   T
D   K   A   S   D   U   B   E   E   F   A
G   W   C   Q   E   P   G   C   A   B   G
E   O   E   G   E   R   E   D   R   T   N
A   G   E   D   D   M   C   A   G   E   M
M   X   E   H   S   Z   X   O   T   R   Y
L   B   A   G   Y   B   E   A   D   L   M
```

Notes

Words B E D ___ ___ ___ ___ ___ ___ ___ ___

___ ___ ___ ___ ___ ___

Using only letters from the musical alphabet, print the names of the pictures. Then draw the notes on the staff.

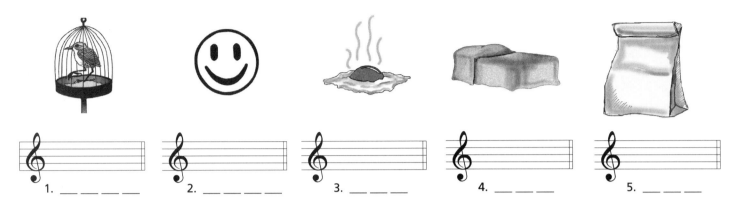

1. _ _ _ _   2. _ _ _ _   3. _ _ _   4. _ _ _ _   5. _ _ _

Complete the crossword puzzle using musical terms.

Across

1) ∨ Symbol for a strum in what direction?

4) The letters of the open guitar strings (lowest to highest)

6) ⊓ Symbol for a strum in what direction?

7) This 𝄞 is a G _____ .

Down

2) The letters used to refer to the fingers on the right hand.

3) The letters of the spaces on the staff (lowest to highest.)

5) The letters of the lines on the staff (lowest to highest.)

Quarter Notes

Now that we know how to use the clef and staff to tell which note to play, we need to know how long each note is held. Every note or chord has a note *value*, or *duration*. Black notes with stems ♩♪ are called *quarter notes,* and receive one beat. Remember, a beat is a basic unit of time. Each beat is like a pulse, or clock ticking.

Time Signature Review

On page 16 you learned that ¼ means there are four beats in a measure. Now that you are learning more about reading music, you can more fully understand the symbol.

4 = Four beats per measure.
4 = A quarter note ♩ gets one beat.

Notes on the 1st String

Here are some notes on the 1st string. This is a good time to review the "Left-Hand Technique" section on page 10.

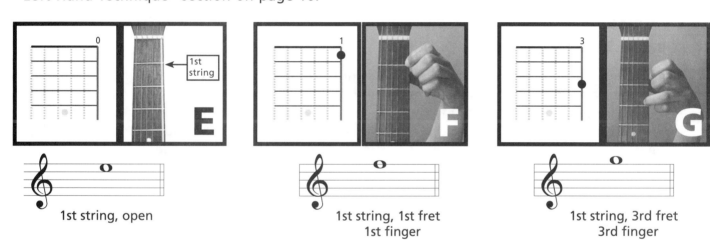

1st string, open

1st string, 1st fret
1st finger

1st string, 3rd fret
3rd finger

1st String Exercise

track 12

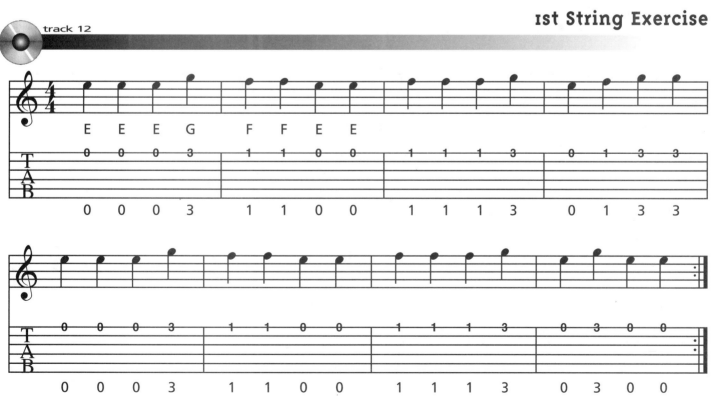

Notes on the 2nd String

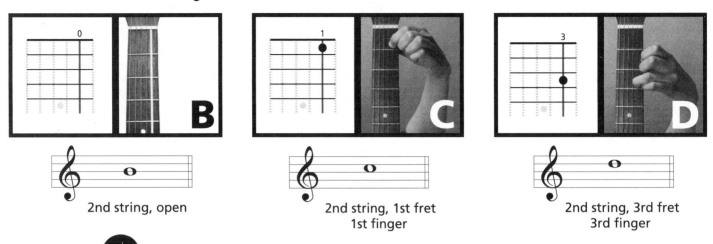

2nd string, open

2nd string, 1st fret
1st finger

2nd string, 3rd fret
3rd finger

Half Notes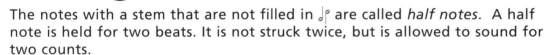

The notes with a stem that are not filled in ♩ are called *half notes*. A half note is held for two beats. It is not struck twice, but is allowed to sound for two counts.

The Quarter Rest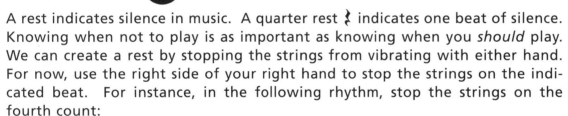

A rest indicates silence in music. A quarter rest 𝄽 indicates one beat of silence. Knowing when not to play is as important as knowing when you *should* play. We can create a rest by stopping the strings from vibrating with either hand. For now, use the right side of your right hand to stop the strings on the indicated beat. For instance, in the following rhythm, stop the strings on the fourth count:

1   2   3   4

2nd String Exercise

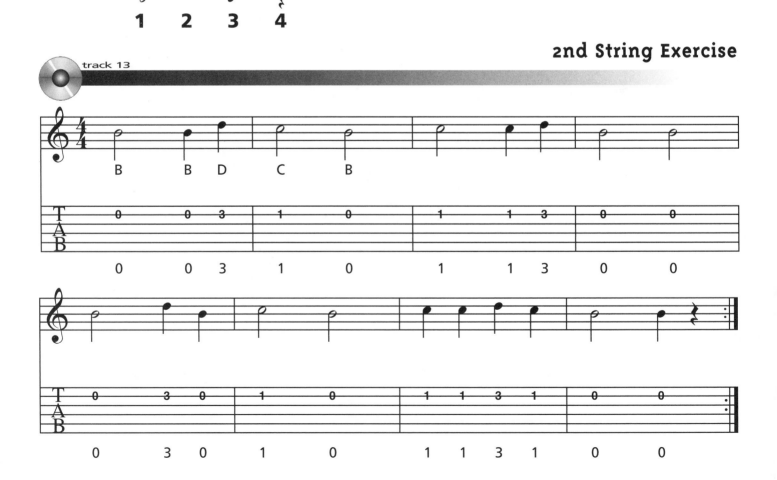

track 13

Whole Notes

Whole notes are not filled in and do not have stems. They last for four beats.

Notice the time signature in *Bee to Gee*. The time signature $\frac{4}{4}$ is so common that it is often referred to as *common time*, and indicated with a $\mathbf{C}$.

Bee to Gee

track 14

These letters indicate the chords that accompany this melody on the DVD audio.
You can also have your teacher or a friend play the chords along with you. Each
chord should be strummed in an even rhythm until a new chord is indicated.

Time Is Ticking

track 15

Notes on the 3rd String

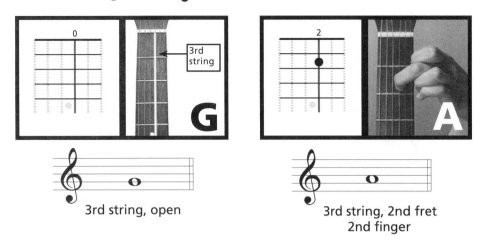

3rd string, open

3rd string, 2nd fret
2nd finger

3rd String Exercise is in $\frac{3}{4}$ time. The top number tells us that there are three beats per measure, and the bottom number reminds us that a quarter note receives one beat.

$\frac{3}{4}$ = A quarter note ♩ gets one beat.

$\frac{3}{4}$ = Three beats per measure.

3rd String Exercise

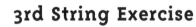

track 16

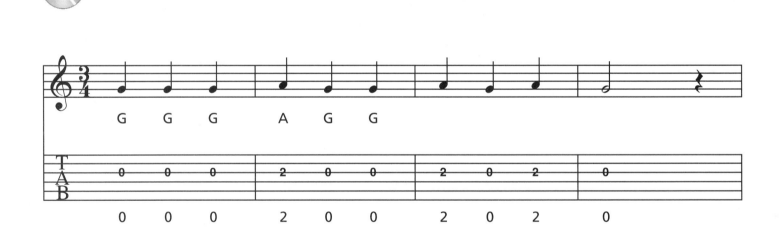

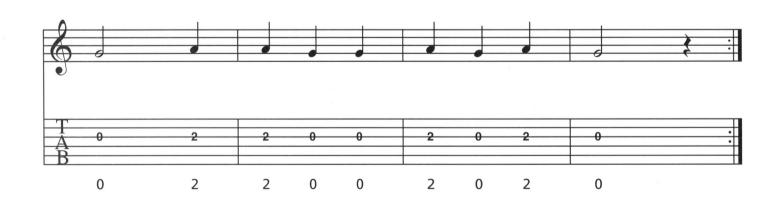

The Half Rest

The *half rest*, which is a black rectangular shape sitting on a line of the staff, indicates two beats of silence. Use the right side of your right hand to mute the strings and create the silence. For instance, in the example below, mute the strings on the third count and remain silent for the fourth.

1 2 3 4

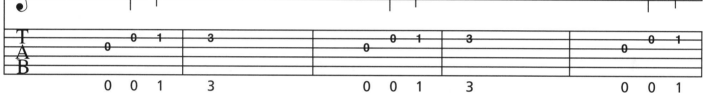

When the Saints Go Marchin' In

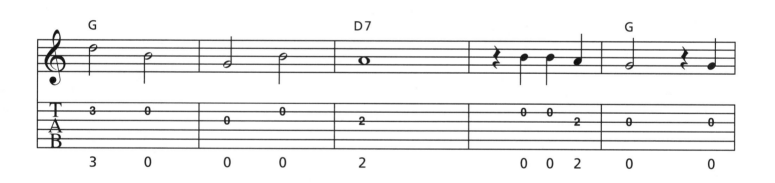

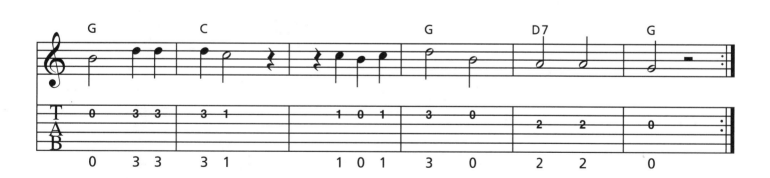

Notes on the 4th String

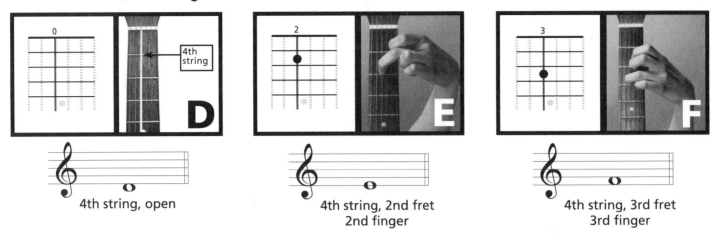

4th string, open

4th string, 2nd fret
2nd finger

4th string, 3rd fret
3rd finger

The Whole Rest

A black rectangle that hangs from a line of the staff is a *whole rest*. This indicates four beats, one full measure in $\frac{4}{4}$ time, of silence.

Dotted Half Notes

A dot next to a note increases its duration by one half. A half note is two beats long, so half of its value is one beat. Add the half notes value to half of its value and you get three beats (2 + 1 = 3). A dotted half note lasts for three beats.

4th String Exercise

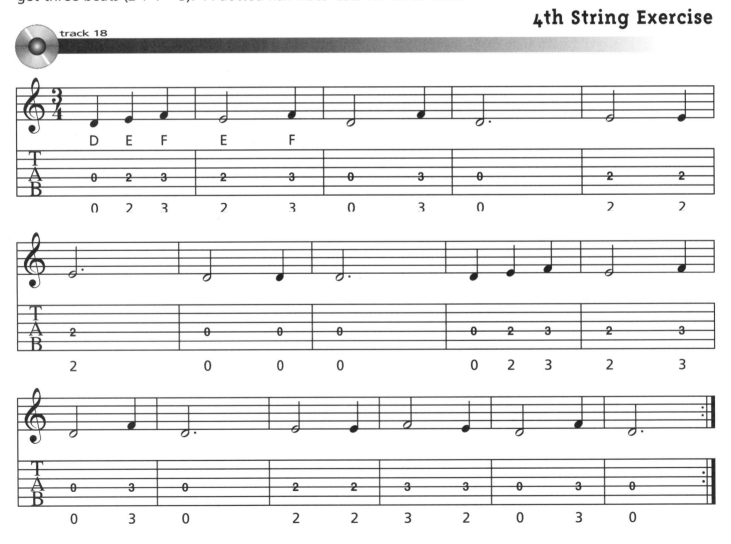

track 18

Eighth Notes

An *eighth note* is filled in and has a flag. Eighth notes receive one half of a beat. Every beat can be divided in half by counting "1 & 2 & 3 & 4 &." The numbers fall on the first half of the beat, and the "&s" on the second. When you tap your foot, the "&" is when your foot comes up. If you play a measure of eighth notes, you play eight notes on the numbers and the "&s."

When eighth notes appear in groups, their flags are *beamed* together:

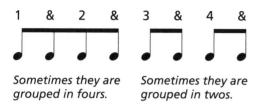

Sometimes they are grouped in fours.   *Sometimes they are grouped in twos.*

Pickup Notes

Pickup notes come before the first full measure of a song. They make up a short, incomplete measure that leads you into the tune. When there is a pickup note, the last measure of the song will also be incomplete, making up for the notes missing in the pickup measure. In *Brahms' Lullaby*, which is $\frac{3}{4}$ time, the first two eighth notes are pickup notes. Count "1 & 2 &," then play on "3" and "&."

Brahms' Lullaby

Ledger Lines

Ledger lines allow us to write notes that are lower or higher than those written on the staff.

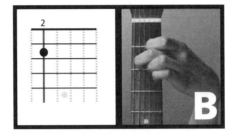

Notes on the 5th String

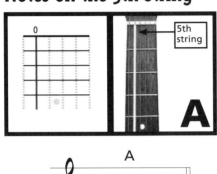

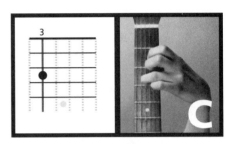

A
5th string, open

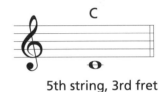
B
5th string, 2nd fret
2nd finger

C
5th string, 3rd fret
3rd finger

Ties

When two notes are *tied* together, play the first note and let it sound for the value of both, without striking the second note. The second note's value is added to that of the first. When a note is tied, the second note in the TAB is in parentheses.

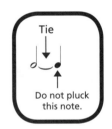
Tie
Do not pluck this note.

5th String Exercise

track 20

A B C B A   B C B C A

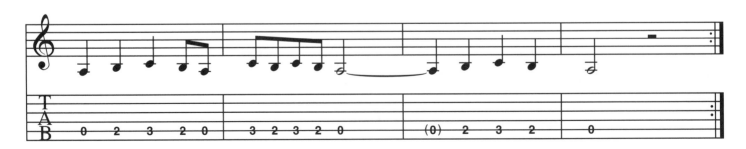

track 21

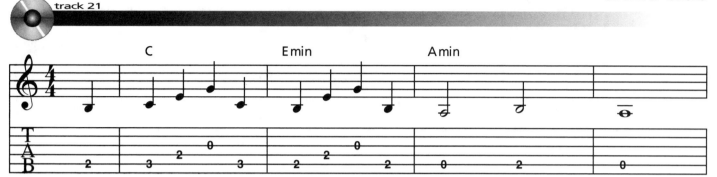

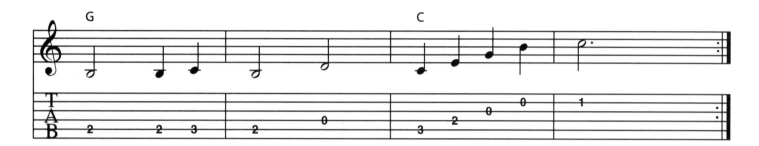

Worksheet #3 (answers on page 71)

Rhythm Review

Place the correct note values in the empty squares to result in a total of four beats on each line.

Look at the time signatures below and complete each measure by adding the number of notes indicated in the circle at the beginning of each line.

1.

2.

3.

4.

Notes on the 6th String

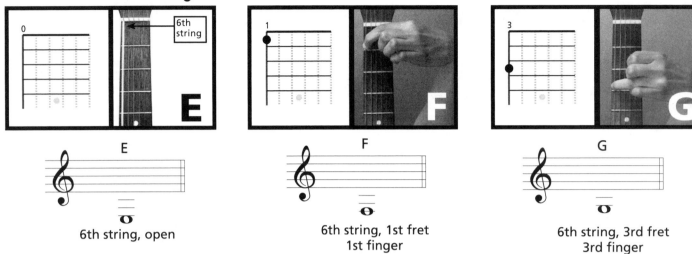

E
6th string, open

F
6th string, 1st fret
1st finger

G
6th string, 3rd fret
3rd finger

6th String Exercise

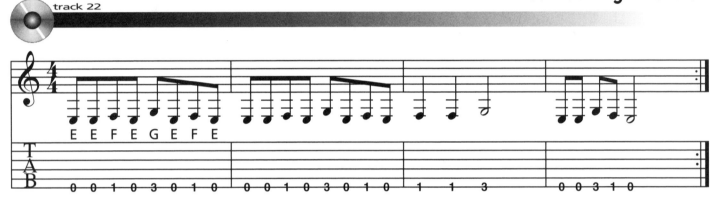

track 22

E E F E G E F E

Accidentals

Accidentals are signs that are used to raise, lower or return a note to its original pitch.

 Sharps raise a note by one *half step* (one fret). For instance, low F is on the 1st fret of th 6th string, so F♯ is on the 2nd fret of the 6th string.

 Flats lower a note by one half step. For instance, low B is on the 2nd fret of the 5th string, so B♭ is on the 1st fret of the 5th string.

 Naturals return a note to its original pitch. Sharps and flats only effect the measure in which they appear. If a note is altered the first time it appears in a measure but not the second time, it is marked with a natural sign.

Ah, But a Man's Reach

track 23

This is your first time using the 4th finger! Just take it slow and practice keeping the finger near the strings.

Boogie in G

track 24

The Major Scale

The *major scale* is the foundation of most of the music that we hear and play. It is probably familiar to you as the tune sung on these syllables: do, re, mi, fa, sol, la, ti, do. A scale is the ordering of notes in a particular sequence of *half steps* and *whole steps.* The major scale consists of eight consecutive notes in alphabetical order with its own unique sequence of whole steps and half steps.

Back on page 38, where accidentals are introduced, you learned that the distance from one fret to the next is called a *half step.* The distance of two half steps is called a *whole step.* If you must skip a fret to go from one note to the next, it is a whole step. A to B, C to D, D to E, F to G and G to A are all whole steps. B to C and E to F are half steps.

Each note in a scale is given a *scale degree* number. The first note is "1" (also called the *root*, or *key note*), the second note is "2," etc. There are whole steps between every scale degree except from 3 to 4 and 7 to 8, which are a half step apart. The root or key note, 1, gives the scale its name and is the most important note. All the other notes revolve around it.

When you play a major scale that starts on C, you are playing in the *key of C Major*. The key of C has no accidentals (sharps or flats). Try playing the C Major scale below. Memorize the sequence of whole steps (W) and half steps (H).

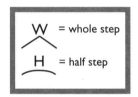

The C Major Scale

track 25

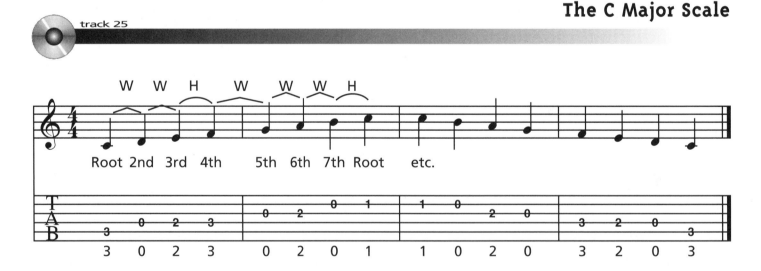

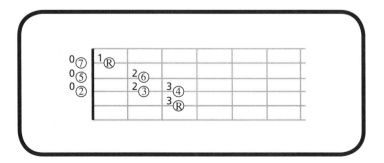

Review:
How the Musical Alphabet Works on the Guitar

As you go up the neck, away from the nut and towards the bridge, the letters go forward in the musical alphabet (A, B, C, D, E, F, G, A, B, C, etc.). Some letters are a whole step apart (two frets) and some are a half step apart (one fret). The half steps are always between B and C, and E and F.

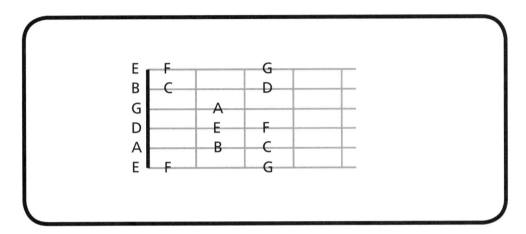

Here is a layout of the first four frets of the fingerboard with the added sharps and flats:

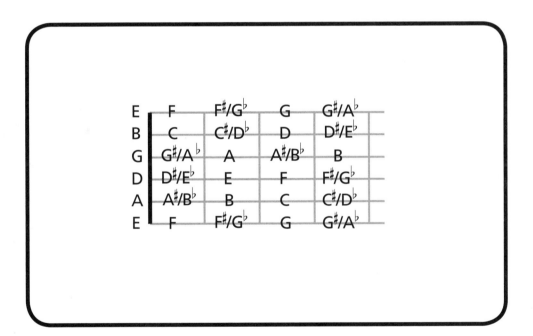

In the diagram above, notice that all the accidentals have two names. Any sharp note can be renamed as a flat note, and vice versa. When two notes sound the same (are played on the same fret) but have different names (are spelled differently), they are said to be *enharmonically equivalent*. For instance, C♯ and D♭ are *enharmonically related*. They are played exactly the same way, and sound exactly the same, but they have different names.

Blues Rhythm Patterns

The blues is a melting pot of several styles of music (African, classical, religious) and cultural influences (African and American) that was born out of the African slave experience in America. It is so ingrained in our culture today that we all know the sound. In fact, popular music as we know it would not exist without its blues roots.

The twelve-bar blues is a standard format for the blues. It is a standard chord progression (sequence of chords) consisting of twelve measures and revolving mostly around just three chords. *Twelve-Bar Blues* on page 43 is in this format.

You have already learned one way to play the A, D and E chords. In the blues there is a another way to play these chords. We can play only the two lower strings of each chord to create a bassy, hollow sound. For a listing of songs played this way, refer to page 70 of this book.

For the A Chord...
only the 5th and 4th strings are played.
The 5th string is played open.
The 1st finger plays the 4th string, 2nd fret and alternates with
The 3rd finger on the 4th string, 4th fret.

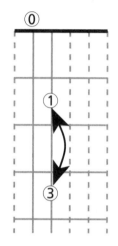

For the D Chord...
only the 4th and 3rd strings are played.
The 4th string is played open.
The 1st finger plays the 3rd string, 2nd fret and alternates with
The 3rd finger on the 3rd string, 4th fret.

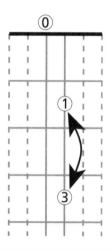

For the E Chord...
only the 6th and 5th strings are played.
The 6th string is played open.
The 1st finger plays the 5th string, 2nd fret and alternates with
The 3rd finger on the 5th string, 4th fret.

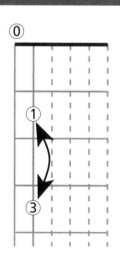

This tune is a standard twelve-bar blues. Enjoy!

track 26

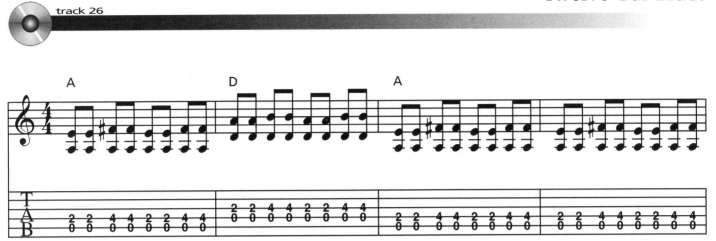

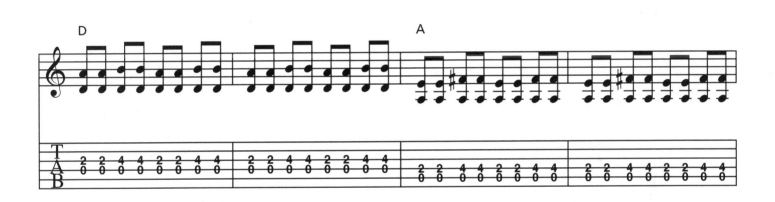

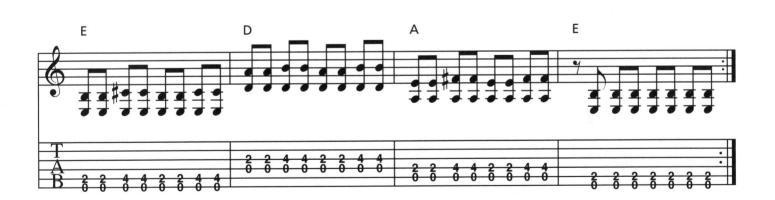

An Introduction to Improvisation

Until now, your goal has been to play exactly what was written on the page as accurately as possible. Although it was musical, it left little to creativity. It would be fun to spontaneously create your own music. That is what improvising is all about.

Improvising is like telling a story by creating your own melody in a solo. A solo is a place in the music where you are the star—the main part. You can put all of your emotions, happy or sad, into your solos.

When we solo, we start with a scale as the foundation. We will start with the five-note *minor pentatonic scale*, which comes to us from Africa and is the most important scale in blues and rock improvisation. The notes may be played in any order, rhythm or combination.

Here is the A Minor Pentatonic scale. Play up and down through the scale and try to memorize the finger pattern, as shown in the diagram, so that you can freely use these notes to improvise.

track 27

A Minor Pentatonic Scale

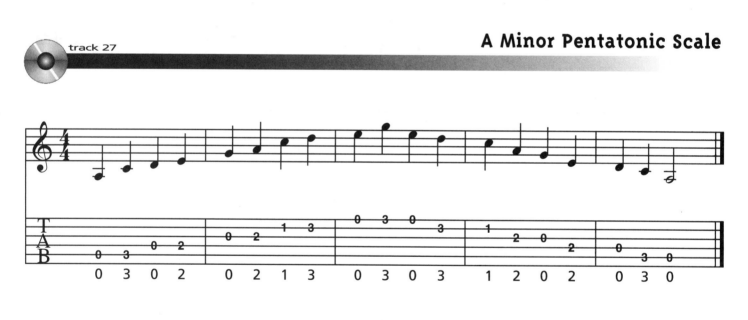

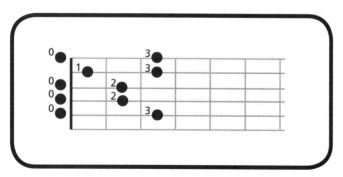

Here is a basic blues solo that has been written out for you. It is based on the A Minor Pentatonic scale. Practice it until you are comfortable with it and are inspired to create a solo of your own. Then, have a friend or your teacher play the chords (or use the DVD audio for this book) while you improvise your solo.

Twelve-Bar Blues Solo

track 28

Review Worksheet

1. Write the location of each note shown in the TAB.

2nd string, 1st fret   1. _____   2. _____   3. _____   4. _____

2. The example below is an excerpt from a well known tune. Using the TAB, and dots (indicating short notes) and lines (indicating long notes), play through each and write down their names.

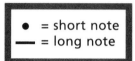

● = short note
— = long note

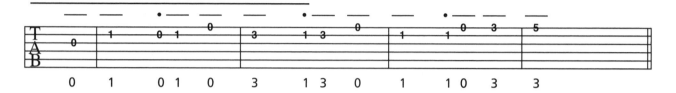

3. Draw the symbols to match their names.

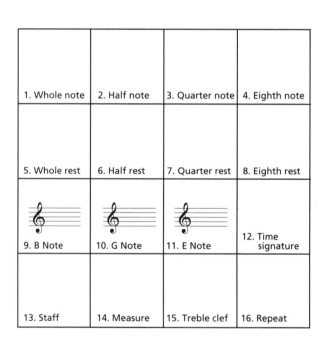

1. Whole note	2. Half note	3. Quarter note	4. Eighth note
5. Whole rest	6. Half rest	7. Quarter rest	8. Eighth rest
9. B Note	10. G Note	11. E Note	12. Time signature
13. Staff	14. Measure	15. Treble clef	16. Repeat

4. Draw the bar lines to make four measures of four beats each.

5. Spell the words that are written on the staff.

sample:

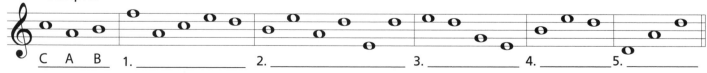

C A B   1. _____   2. _____   3. _____   4. _____   5. _____

Two New Chords: F and Bmin

There are two new chords in the next tune. The first is an F chord. This is your first barre chord. A barre chord is when the 1st finger covers two or more strings. In the F chord, your 1st finger lays down over both the 1st and 2nd strings. It will take a little extra strength to make the notes sound clear, but you can do it.

The F Chord
The 1st finger plays the 2nd string, 1st fret
   and the 1st string, 1st fret.
The 2nd finger plays the 3rd string, 2nd fret.
The 3rd finger plays the 4th string, 3rd fret.
Strum down over the top four strings.

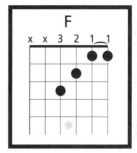

The Bmin Chord
The 1st finger plays the 1st string, 2nd fret.
The 2nd finger plays the 2nd string, 3rd fret.
The 3rd finger plays the 4th string, 4th fret.
The 4th finger plays the 3rd string, 4th fret.
Strum down over the top four strings.

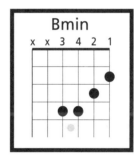

Changes

track 29

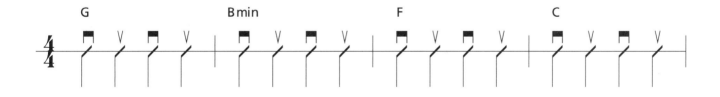

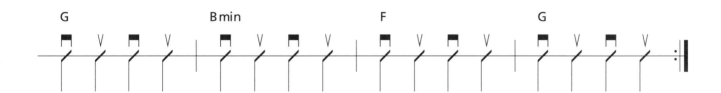

Three New Bluesy Chords: A7, B7 and E7

These chords are all "7th" chords. You will recognize the bluesy character that this type of chord creates.

The A7 Chord
The 1st finger plays the 4th string, 2nd fret.
The 2nd finger plays the 2nd string,
   2nd fret.
Strum down over the top five strings.

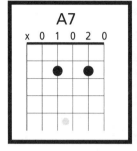

The E7 Chord
The 1st finger plays the 3rd string, 1st fret.
The 2nd finger plays the 5th string, 2nd fret.
Strum down over all six strings.

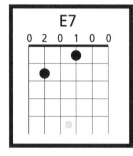

The B7 Chord
The 1st finger plays the 4th string, 1st fret.
The 2nd finger plays the 5th string, 2nd fret.
The 3rd finger plays the 3rd string, 2nd fret.
The 4th finger plays the 1st string, 2nd fret.
Strum down over the top five strings.

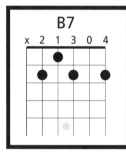

The strum for this song more involved than the others we have been playing. The first note in each measure is a plucked bass note; this is then followed by an up-down-up (Bass ∨ ∎∨) pattern. Also, remember each chord has its own bass note.

True Blue

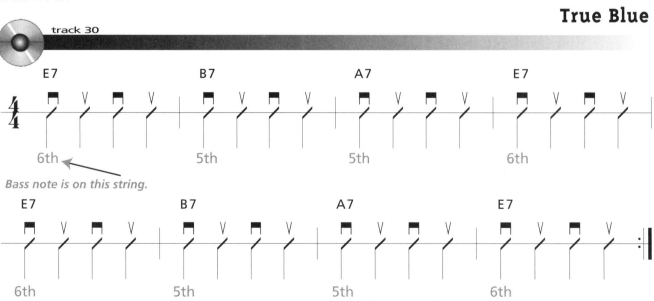

Bass note is on this string.

Review: The Notes on 1st, 2nd and 3rd Strings

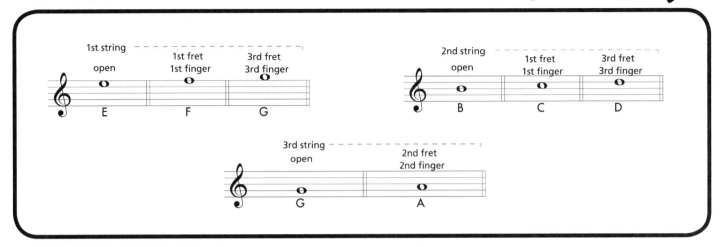

Double Stops and Some New Signs

Double Stops

On the guitar, we often play two notes simultaneously. This is referred to as playing *double stops*. Simply pluck both notes at once with the pick.

1st and 2nd Endings

This song uses 1st and 2nd endings. When you come to the repeat sign (see page 5) go back to the beginning. You will then play up to 1st ending, skip it, and continue on from the 2nd ending to the end of the song.

D. C. al Fine

At the end of the tune you will find the marking *D. C. al Fine*. "D. C." stands for *Da Capo*, which means to return to the beginning. The marking "al fine" means to play up until the *"Fine."* So the whole marking, *"D. C. al Fine,"* means to return to the beginning and play up until the *"Fine"* without repeats.

Notice the eighth notes in the seventh and eighth measures. Count carefully.

Beethoven's 9th

Review: The Notes on 4th, 5th and 6th String

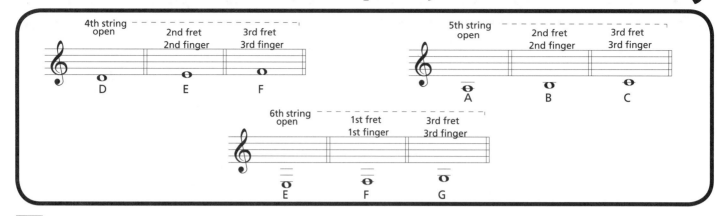

Review: Accidentals

Accidentals are signs that are used to raise, lower or return a note to its natural pitch.

*Sharps* raise a note by one half step (one fret). For instance, low F is on the 1st fret of the 6th string, so F♯ is on the 2nd fret of the 6th string.

♭   *Flats* lower a note by one half step. For instance, low B is on the 2nd fret of the 5th string, so B♭ is on the 1st fret of the 5th string.

♮   *Naturals* return a note to its original natural pitch. Sharps and flats are only in force during the measure in which they appear. If a note is altered the first time it appears in a measure, but not the second time, it is marked with a natural sign.

Bach's Minuet in G

track 32

Enjoy playing either the melody or the chords to this classic song. For strumming the chords, try a bass-strum-bass-strum pattern (bass ⊓ bass ⊓).

Bill Bailey Won't You Please Come Home

track 33

Fingerstyle

Your right hand usually has the job of strumming the guitar. Although the sound is very full, sometimes you need a more delicate sound. An alternative to strumming is *fingerstyle*, or *fingerpicking*. Instead of the notes in a chord being played all at once, they are played individually, or *arpeggiated*. A chord that is played in this manner is called an *arpeggio*.

Each finger on the right hand has a string that it almost always plays.

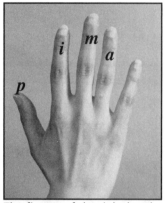

The fingers of the right hand

> *p* ←—**Thumb.** Plays the bass strings: 6th, 5th and 4th.
> *i* ←—**Index finger.** Plays the 3rd string.
> *m*←—**Middle finger.** Plays the 2nd string.
> *a* ←—**Ring finger.** Plays the 1st string.

To strike the strings with the fingers (*i*, *m* and *a*), pull them inward towards the palm. The hand should be still and not pull away from the strings. To play the bass notes with *p*, move the whole thumb as one unit across the string towards the *i* finger. Review Patterns #1 and #2 on page 22, and enjoy warming-up your fingerstyle technique with *Sunday Picnic* below.

Sunday Picnic

track 35

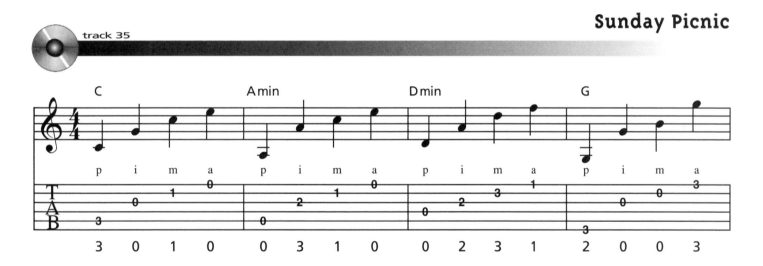

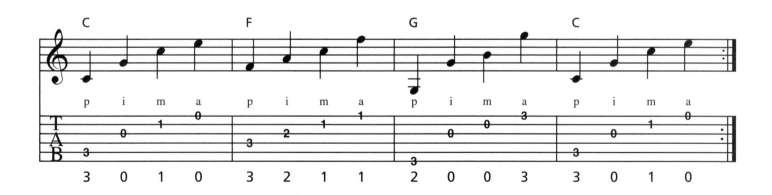

A NEW PATTERN: #3

The beautiful folk song "Scarborough Fair" was made famous by Simon and Garfunkel in the 1960s, is perfectly suited for fingerstyle playing. We will use a new picking pattern in $\frac{3}{4}$ time.

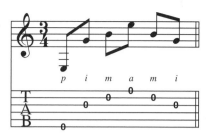

This song introduces a new note: the high A on the 5th fret of the 1st string.

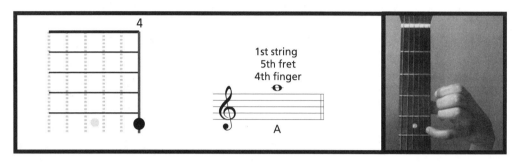

Learn both the melody and the fingerpick (page 55) for this song.

Scarborough Fair-Melody

track 36 - Left Speaker

 track 36 - Right Speaker

Scarborough Fair-Fingerpick

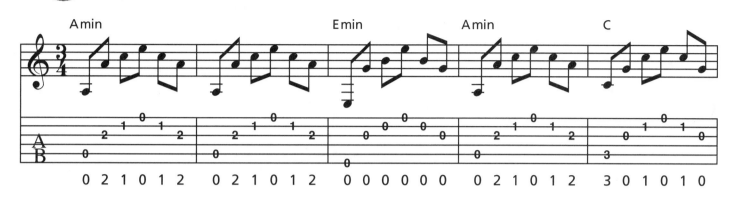

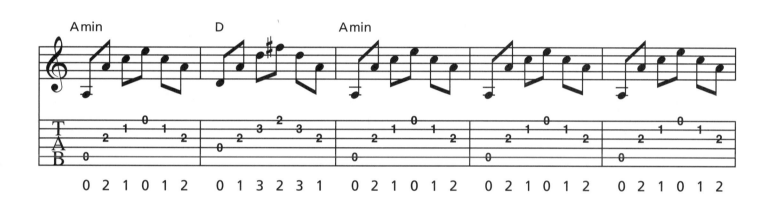

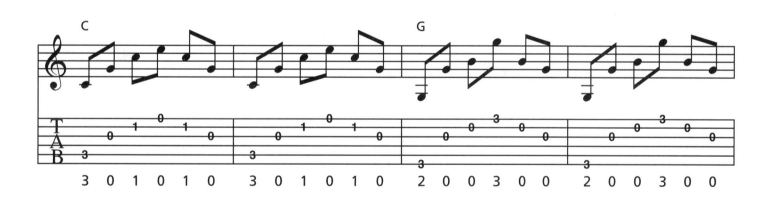

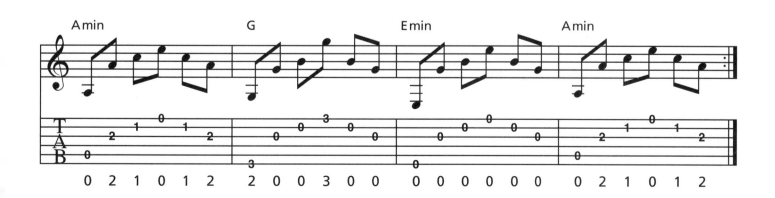

The Natural Minor Scale

Like the minor chords, the minor scale has a sad sounding quality. The minor scale is made up of eight consecutive tones in alphabetical order, just like the major scale, but the half steps are between the 2nd and 3rd and the 5th and 6th scale degrees. The placement of the half steps is what gives this scale its solemn sound.

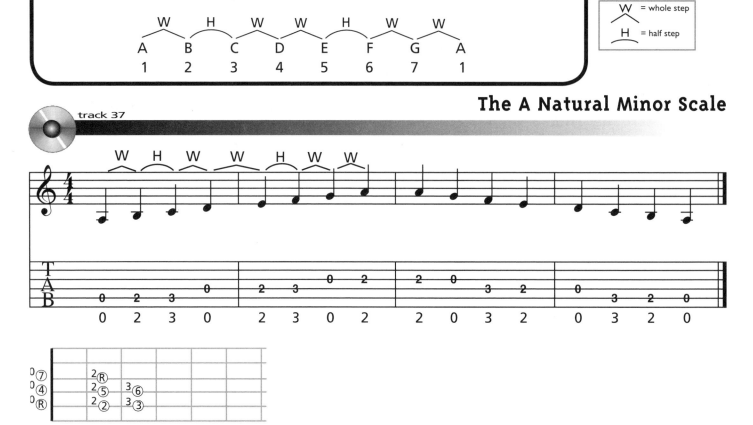

The melody of this next song is taken directly from the natural minor scale.

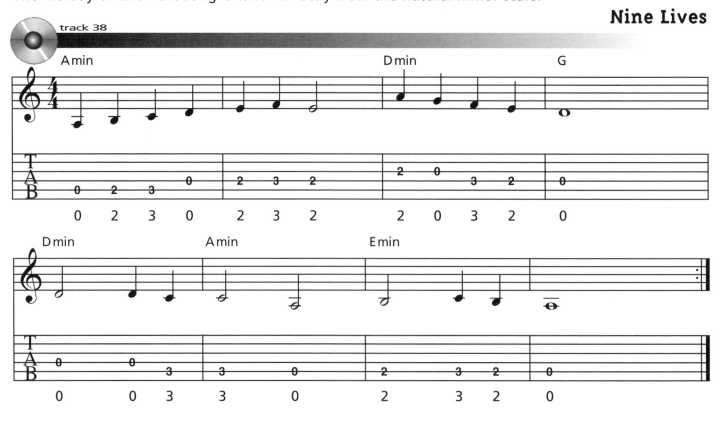

Moveable Chords

Some of the most basic chords that you know can be moved up the neck (to higher numbered frets), keeping the same fingering. The arrangement of notes will remain exactly the same, but the pitch will move up by a half step each fret. The chord quality (major, minor, etc.) will stay the same. We call this kind of chord a *moveable* chord. Any chord that includes no open strings can be a moveable chord. We just need to know where the root of the chord resides in the fingering, and move the chord up to the new, desired root.

For example, look at the diagrams below. At the 1st fret we have an F chord. The F chord does not include any open strings. Remember that an F chord includes a barre across the top two strings (see page 47). The root of the F chord (F) is on the 1st string. If we move it up to the 2nd fret it becomes an F♯ or G♭ chord, because the root at the 2nd fret is a half step higher. At the 3rd fret it becomes a G chord, and so on.

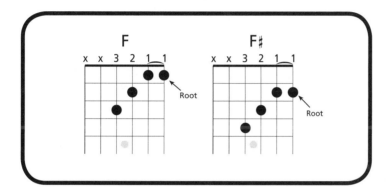

Barre Chords

If a chord does include open strings, it can become a moveable chord by making it a barre chord. To do this, refinger the chord so that the 1st finger is not involved and then moved up the neck to the desired fret. As the chord moves up the neck, the 1st finger lays down behind it over the strings, acting like the nut of the guitar.

It takes practice to make barre chords sound clear. They require working all new muscles in your left hand. Make sure that you are holding the guitar in the proper position. If you find that your hand is getting tired or cramped, take a break. You will get a better tone if you barre with the outside, or left side, of your first finger. It is also very helpful to move your left elbow in, closer to your side. Also, be sure never to barre more strings than is necessary for the chord. But the best tip is to practice, practice, practice!

The E Form Barres

The E chord is one of the most commonly used chords for creating barre chords. Since the 1st finger is needed for the barre, we form the E chord with the other three fingers (2, 3 and 4). The root of this chord is on the 6th string. As the chord moves up the neck, so does the name of the chord. Since the root is on the 6th string, we can call this kind of barre a *Root 6 barre*.

The diagram below shows all the notes on the first twelve frets of the 6th string. These are the roots for the Root 6 chords.

Root 6 Names for E Form Barres

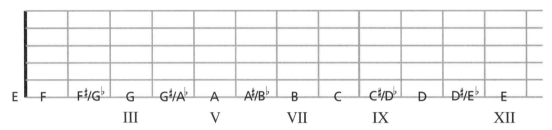

Let's make sure you know the four basic E form chords: E, E7, Emin and Emin7. Let's finger them with the 1st finger free to become a barre. Then, let's move them up one fret to become F, F7, Fmin and Fmin7.

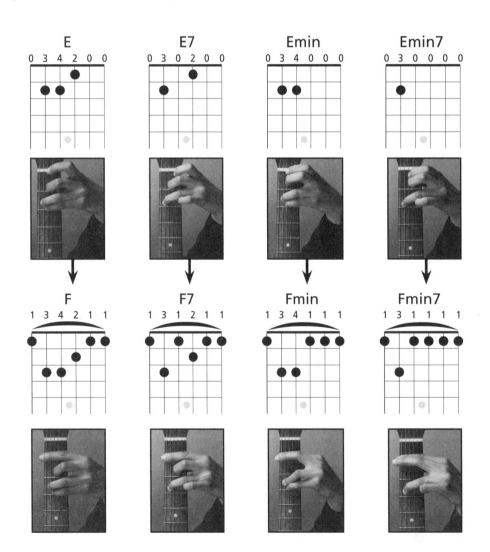

The A Form Barres

The A chords can be used as barres in the same manner as the E chords. First, however, we have to learn the locations of the A roots. Since, in an A chord, the root is on the 5th string, this type of barre can be called a *Root 5 barre*.

The diagram below shows all the notes on the first twelve frets of the 5th string. These are the roots for the Root 5 chords.

Root 5 Names for A Form Barres

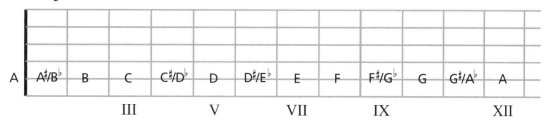

Let's make sure you know the four basic A form chords: A, A7, Amin and Amin7. Let's finger them with the 1st finger free to become a barre. Then, let's move them up one fret to become B♭, B♭7, B♭min and B♭min7. Be patient and have fun!

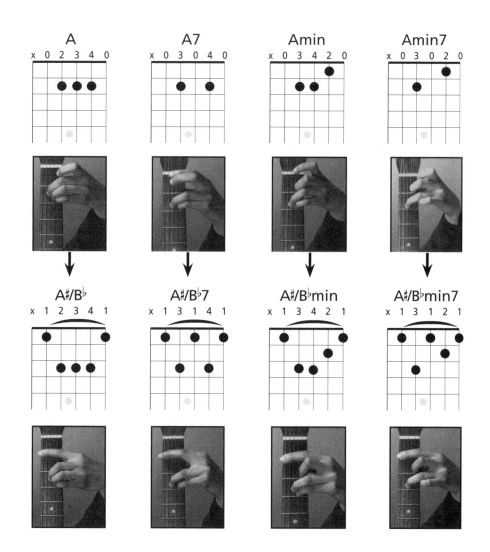

Lessons Learned uses five barre chords: G, Bmin7, Amin, D7 and C (shown below). Practice switching between them before you try putting them together in the song. Strum down four times in each measure. If there are two chords in the measure, strum twice on each.

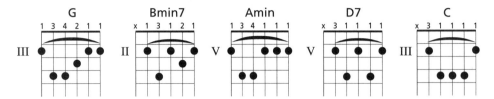

Once you have mastered the chords, enjoy playing the melody, too.

Lessons Learned

track 39

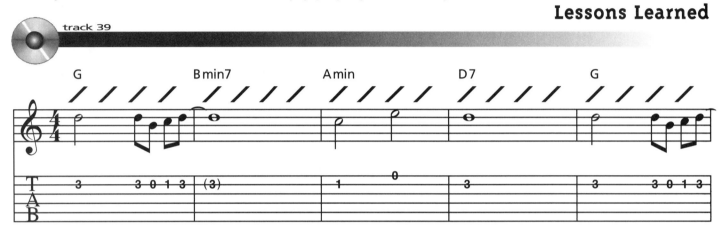

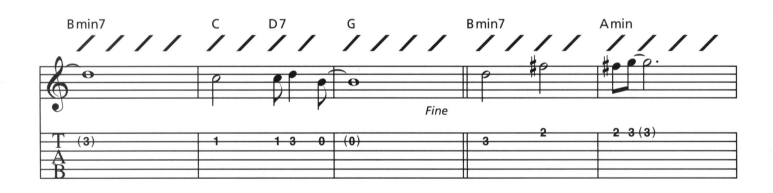

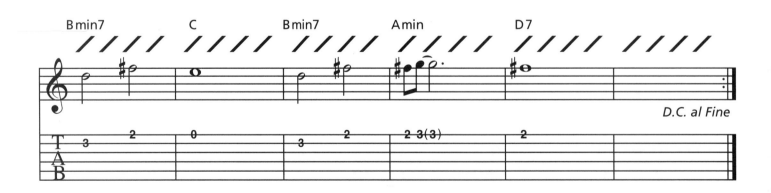

Improvising: The Moveable Minor Pentatonic Scale

When musicians improvise, they start with a scale as the foundation. Earlier, you learned the A Minor Pentatonic scale in the open position. In other words, the scale included open strings. In this book, we will start with the minor pentatonic scale on the 5th fret. It does not include any open strings, and so, like moveable chords, can be moved around the neck to the different roots shown on page 58.

The note that the first finger plays on the 6th string is the root of the scale. Since we will be playing on the 5th fret, and the note on the 5th fret of the 6th string is an A, we will be playing the A Minor Pentatonic scale. The notes in the scale may be played in any order, rhythm or combination.

To play this scale on the 5th fret, you will have to play some familiar notes in unfamiliar places. Use the TAB and the scale diagram to learn these new locations. Congratulations! You are movin' on up the neck.

You will need to learn one new note for this scale: high C on the 8th fret of the 1st string.

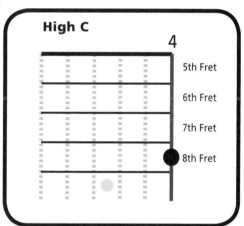

The Moveable A Minor Pentatonic Scale

track 40

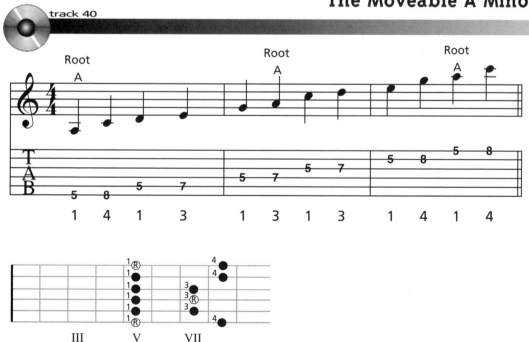

Learn the sample solo provided in *Twelve-Bar Blues Jam* below. The solo is based on the A Minor Pentatonic scale. Notice that the melody in the first measure is repeated a few times. This kind of repetition is a common device for building a solo.

Dotted Quarter Notes

Remember that a dot adds half the value of the note to the existing note value. A quarter note equals one beat (1). So, the dot will equal half of a beat (½). A dotted quarter note will receive one and a half beats (1 + ½ = 1½). This is the same as a quarter note tied to an eighth.

Play the following rhythms on the open 1st string. Count aloud.

Twelve-Bar Blues Jam

Soloing with the Major Scale

There's lots you can do to make your solos interesting. Remember, the notes of the minor pentatonic scale may be played in any order or rhythm. Use your ear and play what sounds good to you. Here are some techniques you can use that will add interest, too.

Notice that the examples on this page are in $\frac{2}{4}$ time—they have two beats per measure.

Hammer-ons

A *hammer-on* creates a special, *legato* (smooth, connected) sound because it involves playing a note that has not been plucked by the right hand. To perform a hammer-on, pluck the first note and then hammer down on a higher note of the same string with another finger of the left hand. The action of tapping the vibrating string with the left hand causes a new note to sound—you do not pluck the second note. Hammer-ons are indicated with a *slur sign* (⌣ or ⌢) between two ascending notes and the letter H above the TAB.

H = Hammer-on

Pull-offs

A *pull-off* is performed by placing two fingers on the same string, then plucking the higher note and pulling the left-hand finger away from the string in a slightly downward direction (towards the floor) thus causing the lower note to sound. The second, lower note is not plucked. This creates a legato sound like the hammer-on, but from a higher to a lower note. Pull-offs are indicated with a slur sign between two descending notes and the letter P above the TAB.

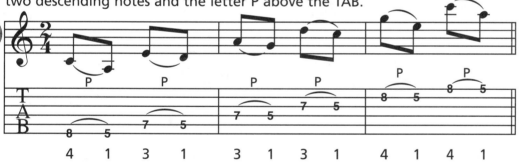

P = Pull-off

Slides

A *slide* is another great way to make a legato connection between notes. To perform a slide, pluck a note, then slide your left hand finger up or down the neck to another note. Keep enough pressure on the string so that the note continues to ring, but not so much that your hand feels rigid. The slides in the example below all involve sliding from a fret below a C Major scale tone up into a scale tone.

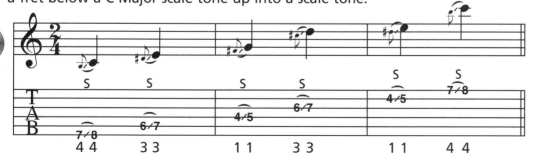

S = Slide

Triplets

A *triplet* is what happens when three notes are played in the time two notes are usually played. For instance, eighth notes divide one beat into two equal parts. In an *eighth-note triplet*, a beat is divided into three equal parts. Here is how an eighth-note triplet is counted:

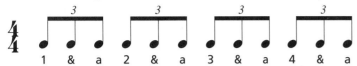

Think of it as a three syllable word like, won-der-ful or tri-pa-let.

Swinging the Eighths, or Shuffle Feel

If you play on only the first and the third part of a triplet (for instance, "1" and "a") you will be playing in *swing* or *shuffle* feel. This is very important for playing blues, jazz, blues-based folk and rock songs.

Usually, the shuffle rhythm will not be written out. The eighth notes are written like regular "straight eighths" (see *Shuffle Solo* below). Musicians will automatically "swing the eighths" when playing a blues-based or jazz tune. Here's how to count to count the shuffle feel:

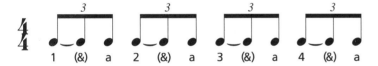

This solo uses all of the techniques that you have just learned. Play the eighth notes with a swing or shuffle feel. Have fun!

Shuffle Solo

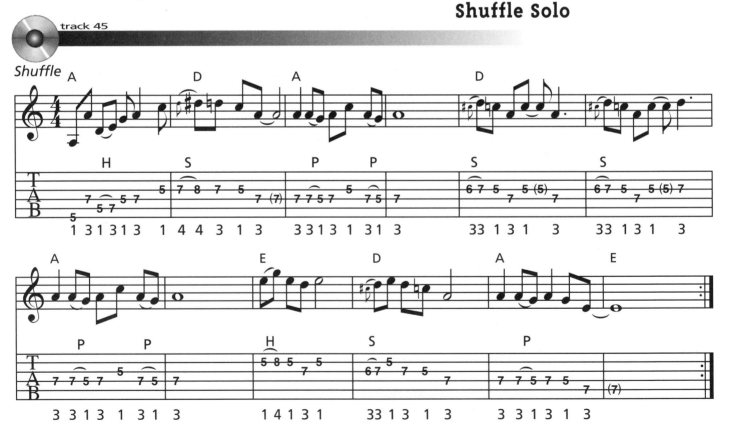

track 45

Understanding the Twelve-Bar Blues

The blues is a melting pot of several styles of music (African, classical, religious) and cultural influences (African and American) that was born out of the African slave experience in America. It is so ingrained in our culture today that we all know the sound. In fact, popular music as we know it would not exist without its blues roots.

The twelve-bar blues is a standard format for the blues. It is a standard chord progression (sequence of chords) consisting of twelve measures and revolving mostly around just three chords, I, IV and V. These are the chords built on the first, fourth and fifth notes of the major scale. For instance, below are the notes of the C Major scale. If we label each note with a Roman numeral (musicians use Roman numerals to identify the chords in a key), we will find that I is a C chord, IV is an F chord and V is a G chord. Just in case it has been awhile since you last used Roman numerals, the chart below shows the Arabic equivalents for each one.

Key of C:	C	D	E	F	G	A	B	C
Roman numerals:	I	II	III	IV	V	VI	VII	I
Arabic equivalents:	1	2	3	4	5	6	7	1

A twelve-bar blues in the key of C will use mostly C, F and G chords.

Twelve-Bar Blues in C

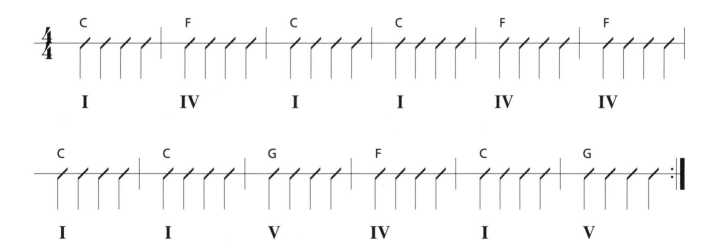

ower Chords

The chords you have learned so far have included three, and sometimes four, different notes. For instance, a major chord is constructed with three different notes of the major scale (the root, 3rd and 5th). You have learned one variation on standard chord playing in the section on Blues Rhythm Patterns (page 42).

Power chords are another variation on chord playing. Like the blues rhythm patterns, they use only two notes from the scale (the root and 5th), but the root is doubled (played twice). These chords produce a heavy, bassy sound, and are favored by many hard rock bands.

Like barre chords (page 57), power chords come in two forms: root 6 and root 5. As with the barre chords, root 6 chords have their root on the 6th string, but it is doubled on the 4th string. Root 5th chords have their roots on the 5th string, doubled on the 3rd.

The diagrams below show both kinds of power chord.

Root on the 6th   Root on the 5th

x = Do not play this string

Power chords are shown with the root followed by the number 5.

A5 = A power chord

As with the barre chords, whatever note your 1st finger plays denotes the name of the chord. Here is a review of the notes on the the 5th and 6th strings.

Notes on the 5th String

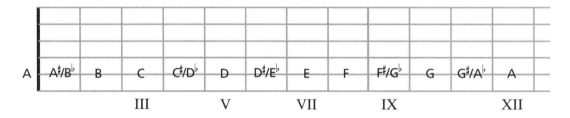

Notes on the 6th String

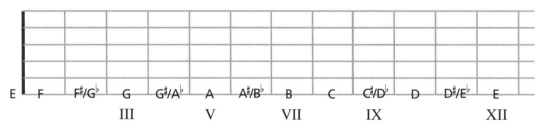

Here are two hard rock songs. They both use these four power chords.

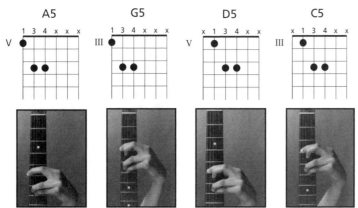

Traffic Jam

track 46

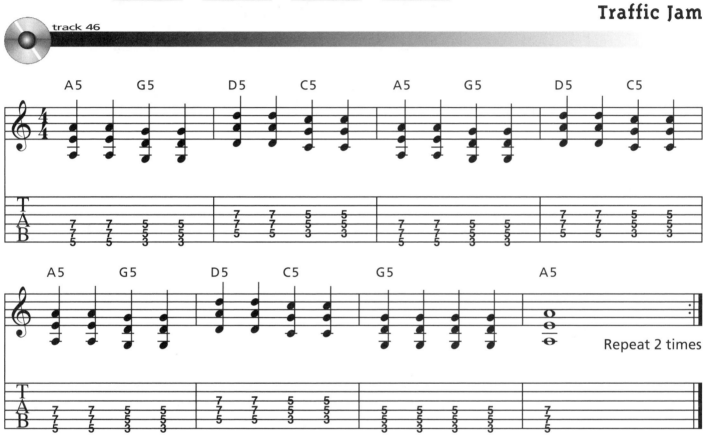

Repeat 2 times

Power Trip

track 47

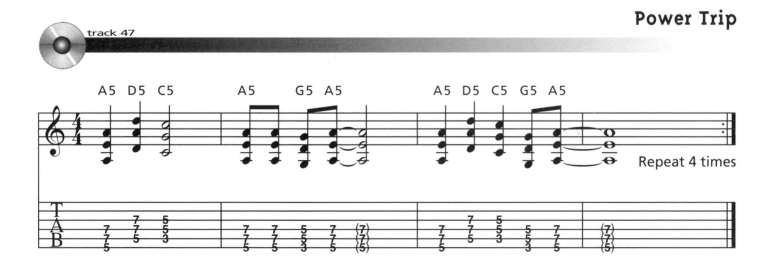

Repeat 4 times

Commonly Used Chords

Here is a chart of chords used in many popular songs.

A
x 0 1 2 3 0
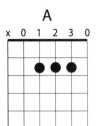

A7
x 0 1 0 3 0
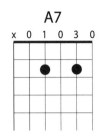

Amin
x 0 2 3 1 0
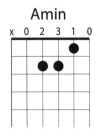

Amin7
x 0 2 0 1 0
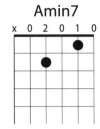

B♭
x x 2 3 4 1

B7
x 2 1 3 0 4
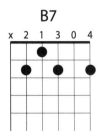

Bmin
x x 3 4 2 1
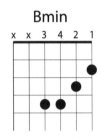

C
x x 2 0 1 0
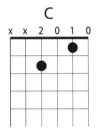

C
x 3 2 0 1 0
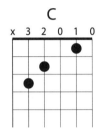

C7
x 3 2 4 1 0
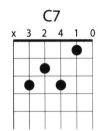

D
x x 0 1 3 2
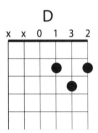

D7
x x 0 2 1 3
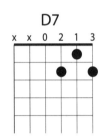

Dmin
x x 0 2 3 1
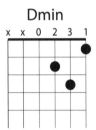

Dmin7
x x 0 2 1 1
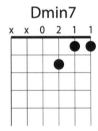

F
x x 3 2 1 1
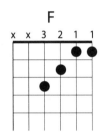

E
0 2 3 1 0 0
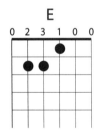

E7
0 2 0 1 0 0
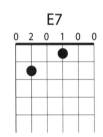

Emin
0 2 3 0 0 0
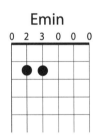

Emin7
0 2 0 0 0 0
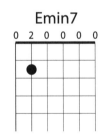

G
x x 0 0 0 3
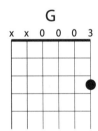

G
2 1 0 0 0 3
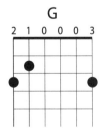

G7
3 2 0 0 0 1
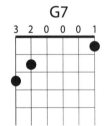

Strums and Picking Patterns

Here is a review of the strums and picking patterns you have learned so far, with a couple of new things thrown in just for fun. Make sure you are familiar with everything on this page.

Strums in $\frac{4}{4}$ Time on an E Chord

track 48 Example #1 | track 49 Example #2 | track 50 Example #3 | track 51 Example #4

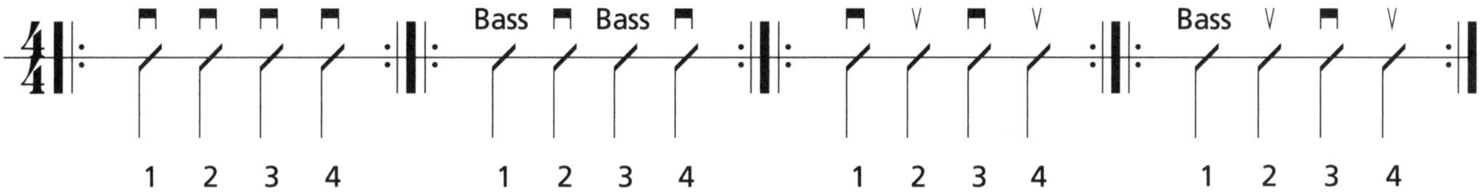

Strums in $\frac{3}{4}$ Time on an E Chord

track 52 Example #5 | track 53 Example #6 | track 54 Example #7 | track 55 Example #8

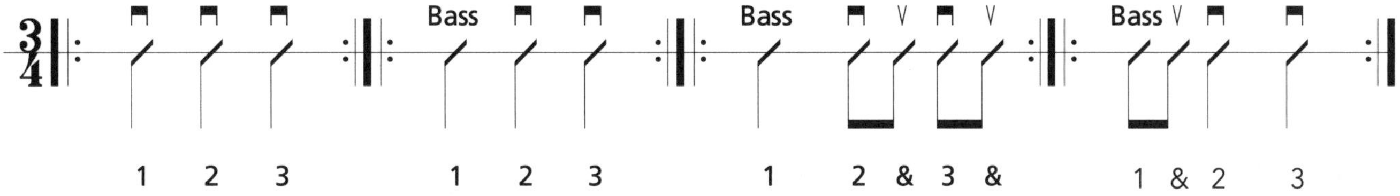

$\frac{4}{4}$ Picking Patterns on an E Chord

track 56 Example #9 | track 57 Example #10 | track 58 Example #11

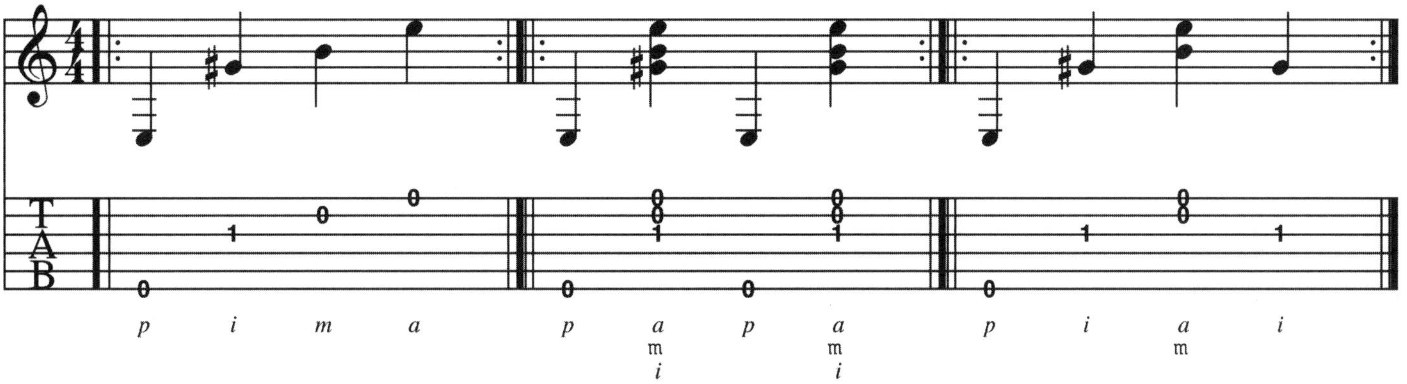

$\frac{3}{4}$ Picking Patterns on an E Chord

track 59 Example #12 | track 60 Example #13 | track 61 Example #14

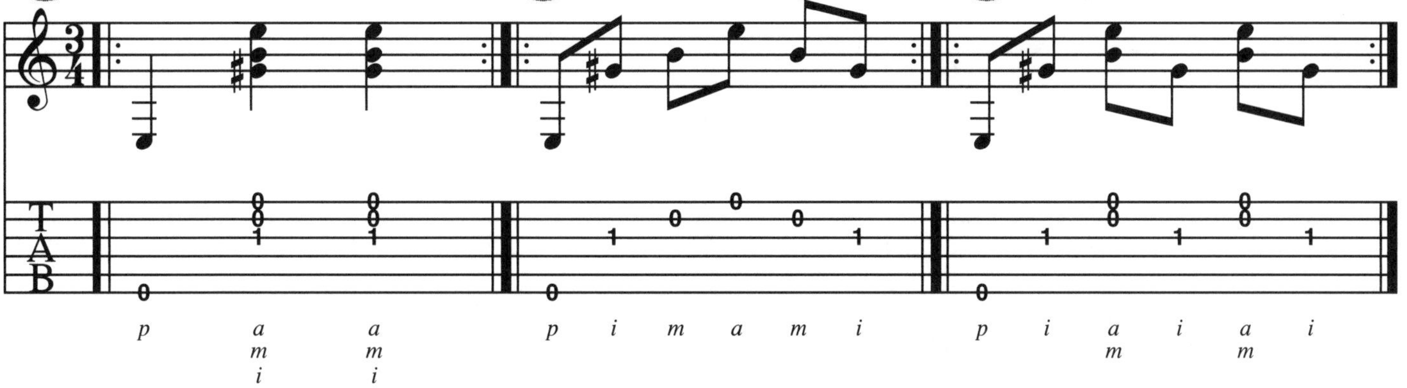

Songs Using A, D and E Chords

There must thousands of songs that can be played with just these three chords. Try these on for size:

Song ●————————● **Artist**

Song	Artist
Amazing Grace	Spiritual
Bad Moon Rising	Creedence Clearwater Revival
Blowin' in the Wind	Bob Dylan
I Wanna Be Sedated	The Ramones
La Bamba	Ritchie Valens
Not Fade Away	Buddy Holly/Grateful Dead
Rockin' in the Free World	Neil Young
Summertime Blues	Eddie Cochran
Sweet Child O' Mine	Guns 'N Roses
Sweet Home Alabama	Lynyrd Skynyrd
The Last Time	The Rolling Stones
Twist and Shout	The Beatles
Wild Thing	The Troggs

Songs Using the Blues Rhythm Pattern

You'll find that all these songs use some variation of the pattern you learned on pages 42 and 43 of this book:

Song ●————————● **Artist**

Song	Artist
Before You Accuse Me	Eric Clapton
Crossroads Blues	Robert Johnson
Ice Cream Man	Van Halen
Johnny B. Goode	Chuck Berry
Pride and Joy	Stevie Ray Vaughan
Rock and Roll	Led Zeppelin
Statesboro Blues	Blind Willie McTell
They Call Me The Breeze	Lynyrd Skynyrd
Truckin'	The Grateful Dead

Songs Using Power Chords

Song ●————————● **Artist**

Song	Artist
China Grove	The Doobie Brothers
Iron Man	Black Sabbath
Mississippi Queen	Mountain
Smells Like Teen Spirit	Nirvana
Smoke on the Water	Deep Purple
Stairway to Heaven	Led Zeppelin
Sunshine of Your Love	Cream
You Really Got Me	The Kinks

Worksheet Answers

Page 19—1

1) Ist string, open
2) 4th string, 2nd fret
3) 3rd string, Ist fret
4) 6th string, 3rd fret
5) 5th string, open
6) 4th string, 4th fret
7) 6th string, open
8) 3rd string, 2nd fret
9) 2nd string, 4th fret

Page 19—2

1) Yankee Doodle
2) Jingle Bells
3) When The Saints Go Marchin' In

Page 27

1) Staff
2) Bar Line
3) Time Signature
4) Guitar
5) Reading Music
6) Beat

Page 27, Musical Alphabet Puzzle

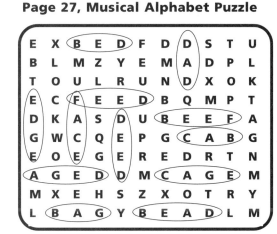

Page 28

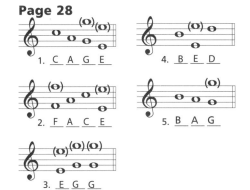

1. C A G E
2. F A C E
3. E G G
4. B E D
5. B A G

Page 28, Crossword Puzzle

1.U	2.P			3.F	
	I			A	
	M	5.E		C	
4.E	A	D	G	B	E
		B			
		6.D	O	W	N
7.C	L	E	F		

Page 37

Notes may be in any order.

Page 37

(music notation exercises 1–4)

(or)

Review Worksheet Answers

Page 46—1

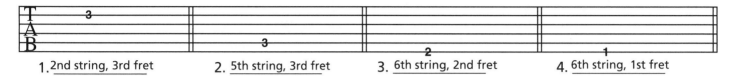

1. 2nd string, 3rd fret   2. 5th string, 3rd fret   3. 6th string, 2nd fret   4. 6th string, 1st fret

Page 46—2

Auld Lang Syne

Page 46—3

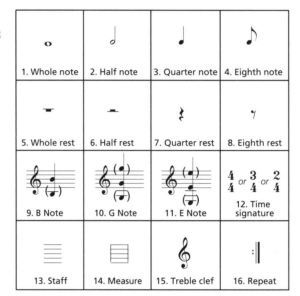

1. Whole note	2. Half note	3. Quarter note	4. Eighth note
5. Whole rest	6. Half rest	7. Quarter rest	8. Eighth rest
9. B Note	10. G Note	11. E Note	12. Time signature
13. Staff	14. Measure	15. Treble clef	16. Repeat

Page 46—4

Page 46—5

1. F A C E D   2. B E A D E D   3. E D G E   4. B E D   5. D A D

Reading Chords

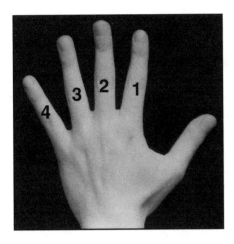

Guitar chord frames are diagrams that contain all the information necessary to play a particular chord. The fingerings, note names and position of the chord on the neck are all provided on the chord frame (see below). The photograph at left shows which finger number corresponds to which finger.

Choose chord positions that require the least motion from one chord to the next; select fingerings that are in approximately the same location on the guitar neck. This will provide smoother and more comfortable transitions between chords in a progression.

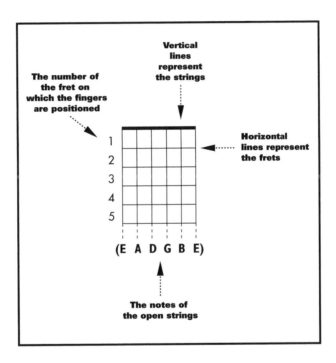

Vertical lines represent the strings

The number of the fret on which the fingers are positioned

Horizontal lines represent the frets

(E A D G B E)

The notes of the open strings

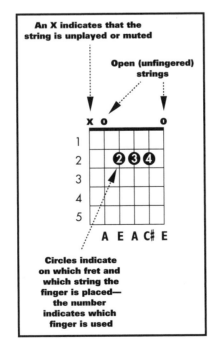

An X indicates that the string is unplayed or muted

Open (unfingered) strings

A E A C# E

Circles indicate on which fret and which string the finger is placed—the number indicates which finger is used

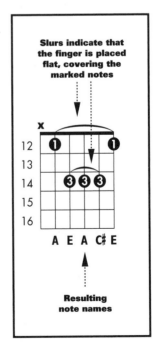

Slurs indicate that the finger is placed flat, covering the marked notes

A E A C# E

Resulting note names

Chord Theory

Intervals

Play any note on the guitar, then play a note one fret above it. The distance between these two notes is a *half step.* Play another note followed by a note two frets above it. The distance between these two notes is a *whole step* (two half steps). The distance between any two notes is referred to as an *interval.*

In the example of the C major scale below, the letter names are shown above the notes and the *scale degrees* (numbers) of the notes are written below. Notice that C is the first degree of the scale, D is the second, etc.

The name of an interval is determined by counting the number of scale degrees from one note to the next. For example, an interval of a 3rd, starting on C, would be determined by counting up three scale degrees, or C-D-E (1-2-3). C to E is a 3rd. An interval of a 4th, starting on C, would be determined by counting up four scale degrees, or C-D-E-F (1-2-3-4). C to F is a 4th.

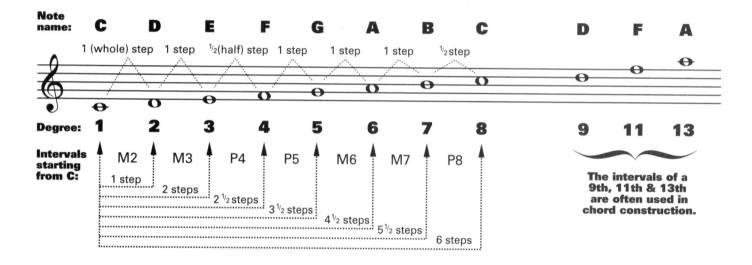

Intervals are not only labeled by the distance between scale degrees, but by the *quality* of the interval. An interval's quality is determined by counting the number of whole steps and half steps between the two notes of an interval. For example, C to E is a 3rd. C to E is also a major third because there are 2 whole steps between C and E. Likewise, C to E♭ is a 3rd. C to E♭ is also a minor third because there are 1½ steps between C and E♭. There are five qualities used to describe intervals: *major, minor, perfect, diminished,* and *augmented.*

M = Major	**o = Diminished (dim)**
m = Minor	**+ = Augmented (aug)**
P = Perfect	

Particular intervals are associated with certain qualities:

2nds, 9ths	= **Major, Minor & Augmented**
3rds, 6ths, 13ths	= **Major, Minor, Augmented & Diminished**
4ths, 5ths, 11ths	= **Perfect, Augmented & Diminished**
7ths	= **Major, Minor & Diminished**

When a *major* interval is made **smaller** by a half step it becomes a *minor* interval.

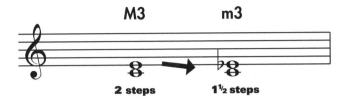

When a *minor* interval is made **larger** by a half step it becomes a *major* interval.

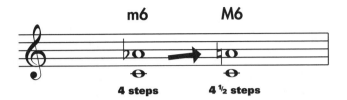

When a *minor* or *perfect* interval is made **smaller** by a half step it becomes a *diminished* interval.

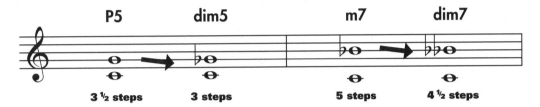

When a *major* or *perfect* interval is made **larger** by a half step it becomes an *augmented* interval.

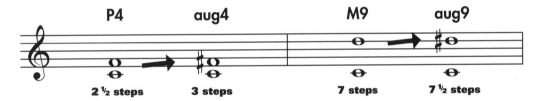

Below is a table of intervals starting on the note C. Notice that some intervals are labeled enharmonic, which means that they are written differently but sound the same (see **aug2** & **m3**).

TABLE OF INTERVALS

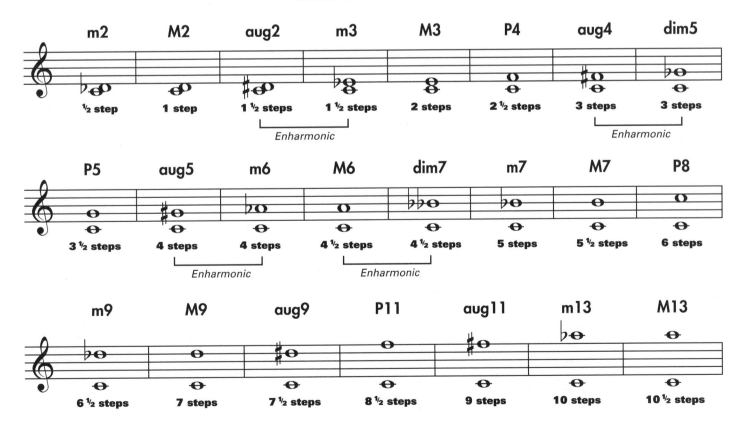

Basic Triads

Two or more notes played together is called a *chord*. Most commonly, a chord will consist of three or more notes. A three-note chord is called a *triad*. The *root* of a triad (or any other chord) is the note from which a chord is constructed. The relationship of the intervals from the root to the other notes of a chord determines the chord *type*. Triads are most frequently identified as one of four chord types: *major, minor, diminished* and *augmented*.

All chord types can be identified by the intervals used to create the chord. For example, the C major triad is built beginning with C as the root, adding a major 3rd (E) and adding a perfect 5th (G). All major triads contain a root, M3 and P5.

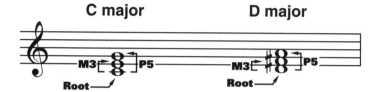

Minor triads contain a root, minor 3rd and perfect 5th. (An easier way to build a minor triad is to simply lower the 3rd of a major triad.) All minor triads contain a root, m3 and P5.

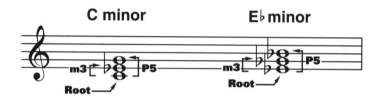

Diminished triads contain a root, minor 3rd and diminished 5th. If the perfect 5th of a minor triad is made smaller by a half step (to become a diminished 5th), the result is a diminished triad. All diminished triads contain a root, m3 and dim5.

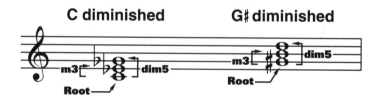

Augmented triads contain a root, major 3rd and augmented 5th. If the perfect 5th of a major triad is made larger by a half step (to become an augmented 5th), the result is an augmented triad. All augmented triads contain a root, M3 and aug5.

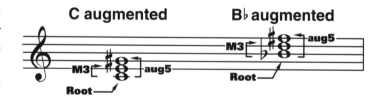

An important concept to remember about chords is that the bottom note of a chord will not always be the root. If the root of a triad, for instance, is moved above the 5th so that the 3rd is the bottom note of the chord, it is said to be in the *first inversion*. If the root and 3rd are moved above the 5th, the chord is in the *second inversion*. The number of inversions that a chord can have is related to the number of notes in the chord: a three-note chord can have two inversions, a four-note chord can have three inversions, etc.

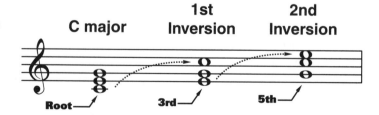

Building Chords

By using the four chord types as basic building blocks, it is possible to create a variety of chords by adding 6ths, 7ths, 9ths, 11ths, etc. The following are examples of some of the many variations.

*The *suspended fourth* chord does not contain a third. An assumption is made that the 4th degree of the chord will harmonically be inclined to *resolve* to the 3rd degree. In other words, the 4th is *suspended* until it moves to the 3rd.

Thus far, the examples provided to illustrate intervals and chord construction have been based on C. Until familiarity with chords is achieved, the C chord examples on the previous page can serve as a reference guide when building chords based on other notes: For instance, locate C7(♭9). To construct a G7(♭9) chord, first determine what intervals are contained in C7(♭9), then follow the steps outlined below.

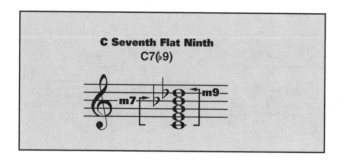

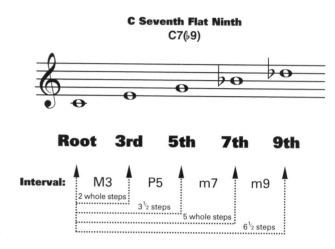

- Determine the *root* of the chord. A chord is always named for its root—in this instance, G is the root of G7(♭9).

- Count *letter names* up from the *letter name of the root* (G), as was done when building intervals on page 96, to determine the intervals of the chord. Therefore, counting three letter names up from G to B (G-A-B, 1-2-3) is a 3rd, G to D (G-A-B-C-D) is a 5th, G to F is a 7th, and G to A is a 9th.

- Determine the *quality* of the intervals by counting whole steps and half steps up from the root; G to B (2 whole steps) is a major 3rd, G to D (3½ steps) is a perfect 5th, G to F (5 whole steps) is a minor 7th, and G to A♭ (6½ steps) is a minor 9th.

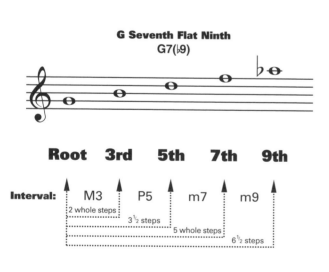

Follow this general guideline for determining the notes of any chord. As interval and chord construction become more familiar to the beginning guitarist, it will become possible to create original fingerings on the guitar. Experimentation is suggested.

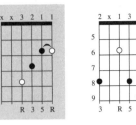

Maj
1, 3, 5

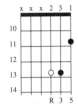

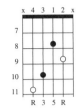

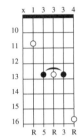
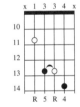

sus2
1, 2, 5

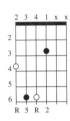

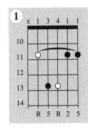
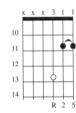

sus4
1, 4, 5

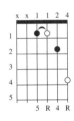

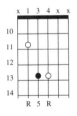

no 3rd
1, 5

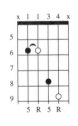

6
1, 3, 5, 6

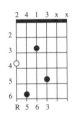

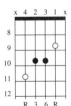

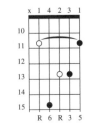

Maj7
1, 3, 5, 7

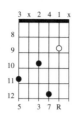 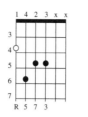 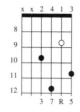   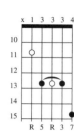

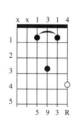  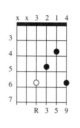   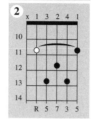

add9
1, 3, 5, 9

 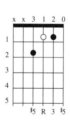   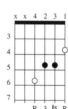

Augmented (aug)
1, 3, ♯5

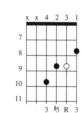 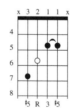 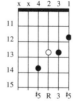

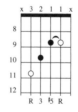

A♭
G♯

 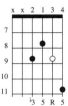 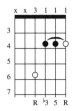 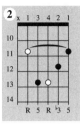   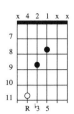 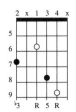 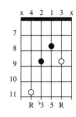

min
1, ♭3, 5

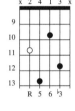 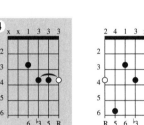 

min6
1, ♭3, 5, 6

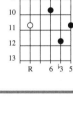 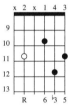 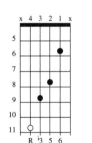   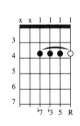

  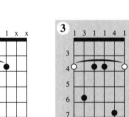 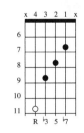 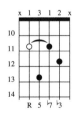 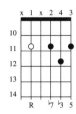  

min7
1, ♭3, 5, ♭7

A♭
G#

7
1, 3, 5, ♭7

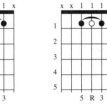
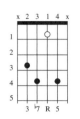

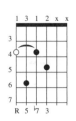
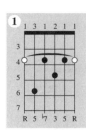

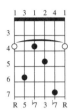
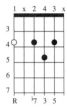

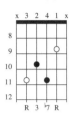

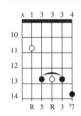
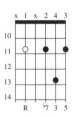

dim7(°7)
1, ♭3, ♭5, ♭♭7

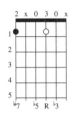
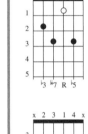
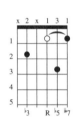

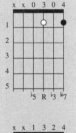

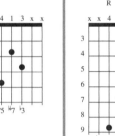
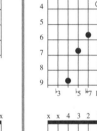

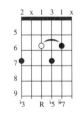
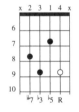
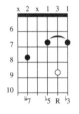

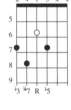

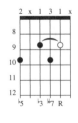
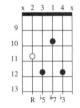
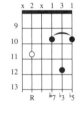
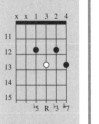
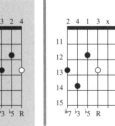
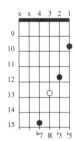

A♭
G#

Maj
1, 3, 5

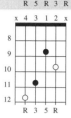
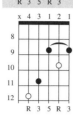
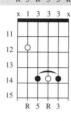

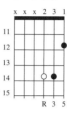

sus2
1, 2, 5

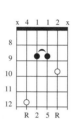
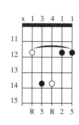
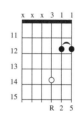

sus4
1, 4, 5

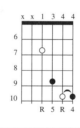
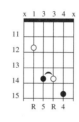

no 3rd
1,5

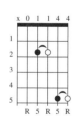

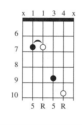

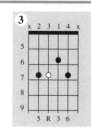

6
1, 3, 5, 6

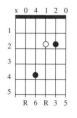
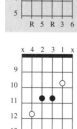
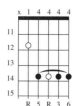
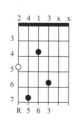
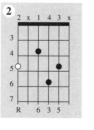
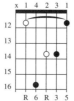

A

Maj7
1, 3, 5, 7

   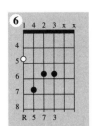 

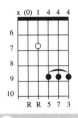 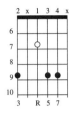 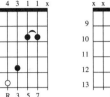 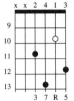 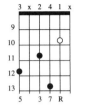 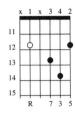

  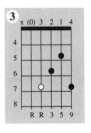  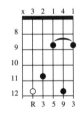 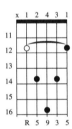

add9
1, 3, 5, 9

 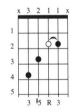   

Augmented (aug)
1, 3, ♯5

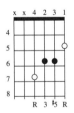 

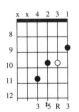 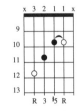

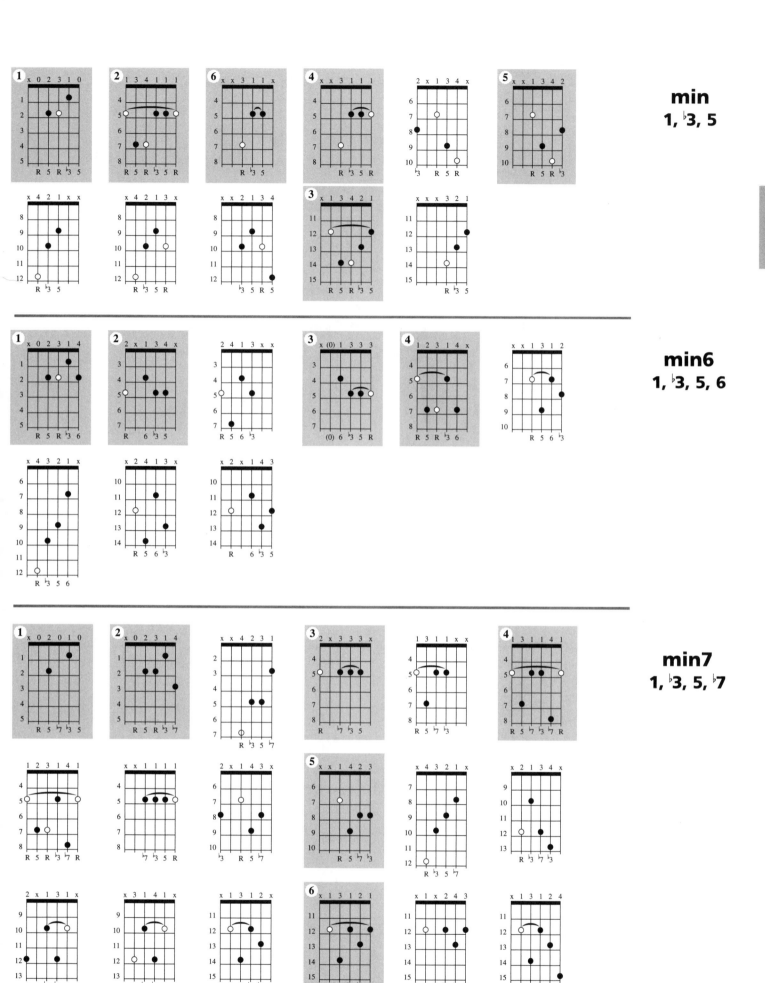

min
1, ♭3, 5

A

min6
1, ♭3, 5, 6

min7
1, ♭3, 5, ♭7

A

7
1, 3, 5, ♭7

 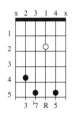 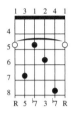 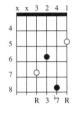 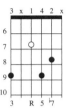 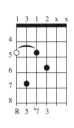

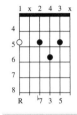 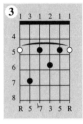 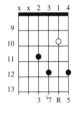 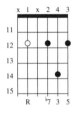 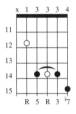 

 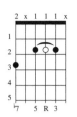   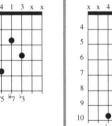 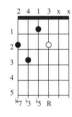

dim7(°7)
1, ♭3, ♭5, ♭♭7

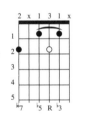 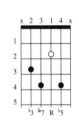 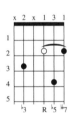  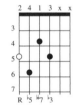 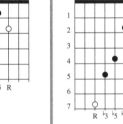

 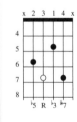 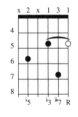   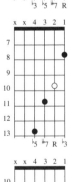

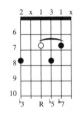 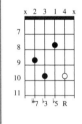 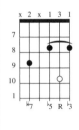 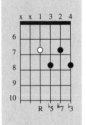  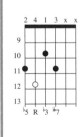

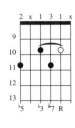 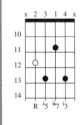 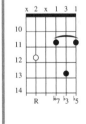

B♭/A♯

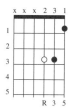   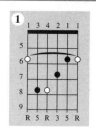 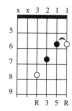

Maj
1, 3, 5

 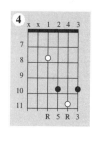  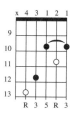

sus2
1, 2, 5

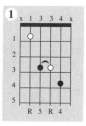 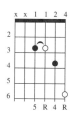  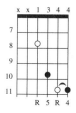 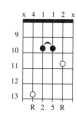

sus4
1, 4, 5

  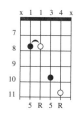

no 3rd
1, 5

B♭
A♯

   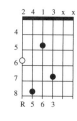  

6
1, 3, 5, 6

  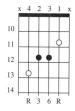

Maj7
1, 3, 5, 7

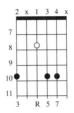

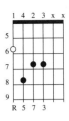

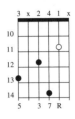
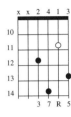

---

add9
1, 3, 5, 9

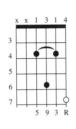

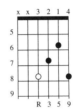
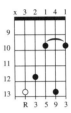

Augmented (aug)
1, 3, ♯5

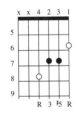

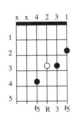

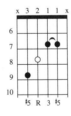

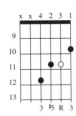

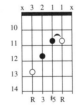

B♭
A♯

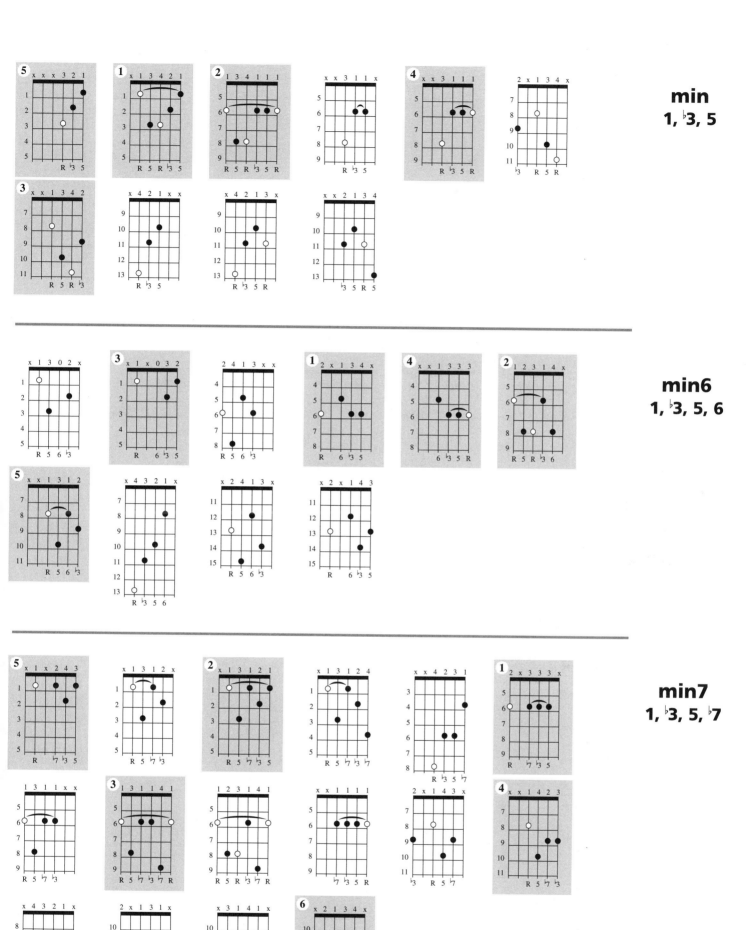

min
1, ♭3, 5

min6
1, ♭3, 5, 6

B♭
A#

min7
1, ♭3, 5, ♭7

7
1, 3, 5, ♭7

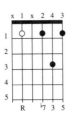  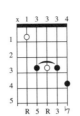   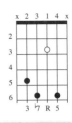

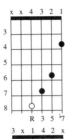 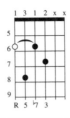    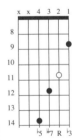

  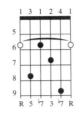 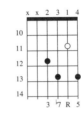

dim7(°7)
1, ♭3, ♭5, ♭♭7

 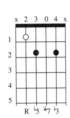 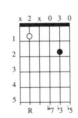 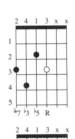  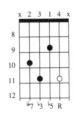

 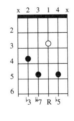   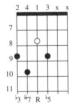 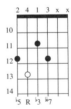

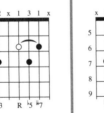  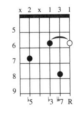 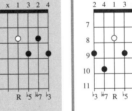 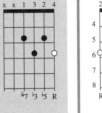 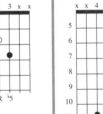

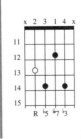 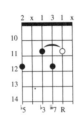 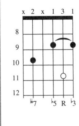 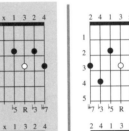 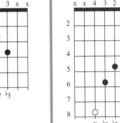 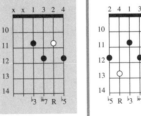

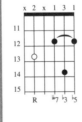 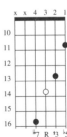

B♭
A♯

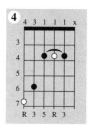
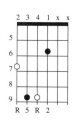

Maj
1, 3, 5

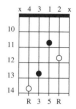
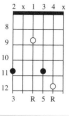
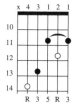
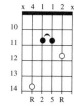

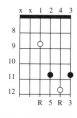
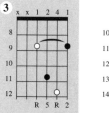
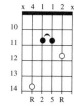

sus2
1, 2, 5

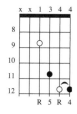
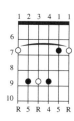

sus4
1, 4, 5

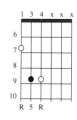
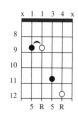

no 3rd
1, 5

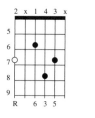

6
1, 3, 5, 6

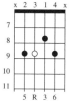
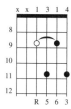
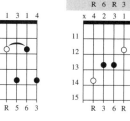

Maj7
1, 3, 5, 7

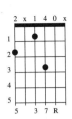

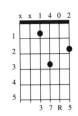

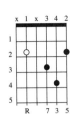

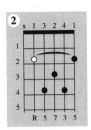

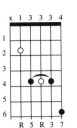

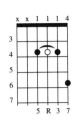

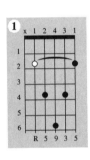

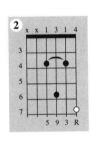

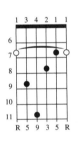

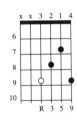

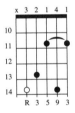

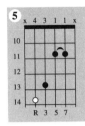

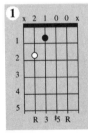

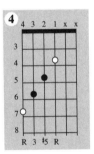

add9
1, 3, 5, 9

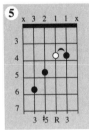

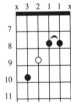

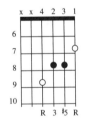

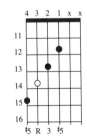

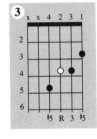

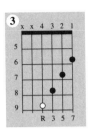

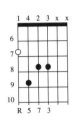

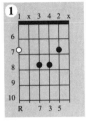

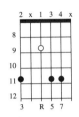

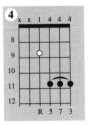

Augmented (aug)
1, 3, ♯5

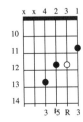

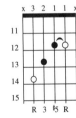

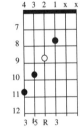

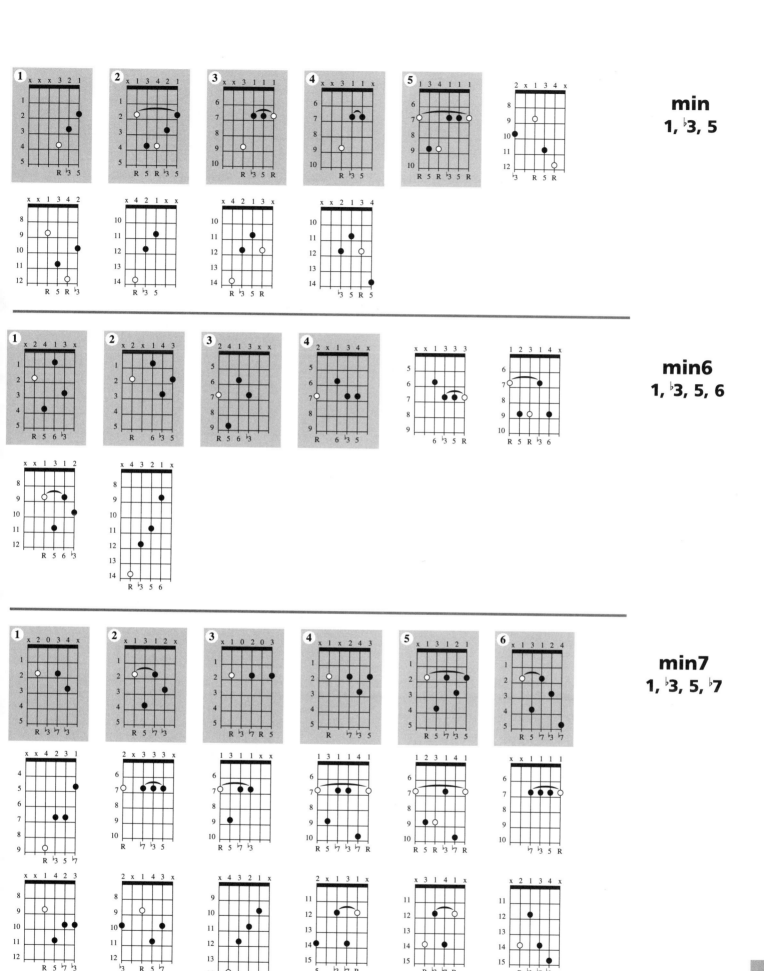

min
1, ♭3, 5

min6
1, ♭3, 5, 6

min7
1, ♭3, 5, ♭7

B

7
1, 3, 5, ♭7

dim7(°7)
1, ♭3, ♭5, ♭♭7

B

C

    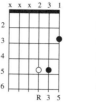 

Maj
1, 3, 5

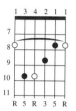 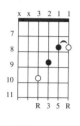 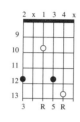  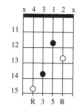 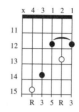

    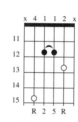 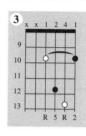

sus2
1, 2, 5

   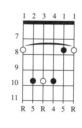 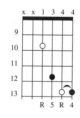

sus4
1, 4, 5

 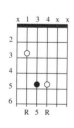 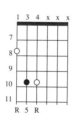 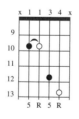

no 3rd
1,5

 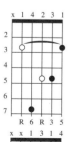 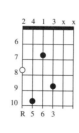   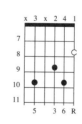

6
1, 3, 5, 6

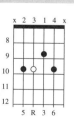 

C

Maj7
1, 3, 5, 7

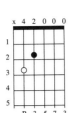    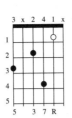 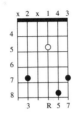 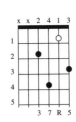 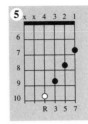 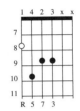   

  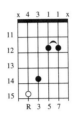   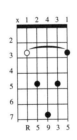 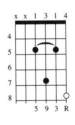  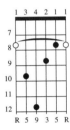

 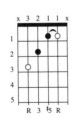 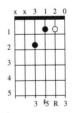

add9
1, 3, 5, 9

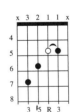 

Augmented (aug)
1, 3, ♯5

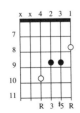 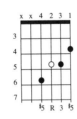  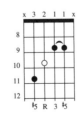 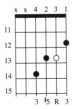

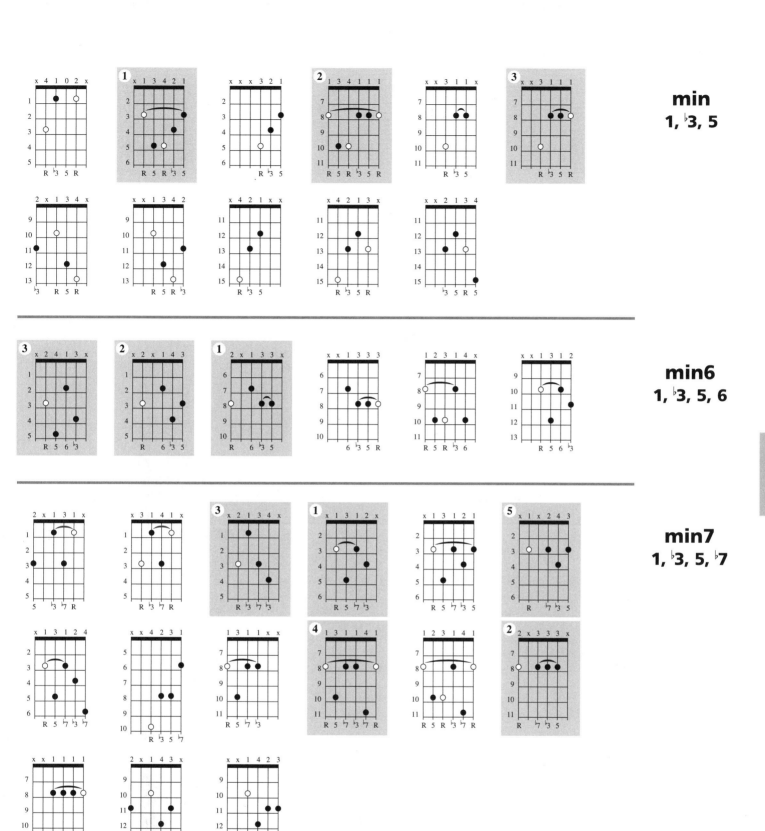

min
1, ♭3, 5

min6
1, ♭3, 5, 6

min7
1, ♭3, 5, ♭7

C

7

1, 3, 5, ♭7

 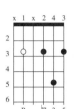   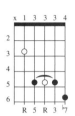 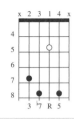

  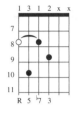 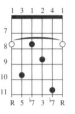  

 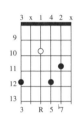  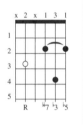

C

dim7(°7)

1, ♭3, ♭5, ♭♭7

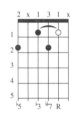 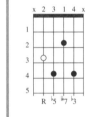 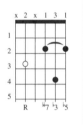   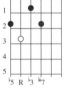

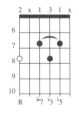    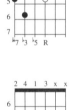 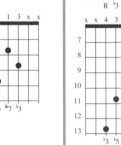

 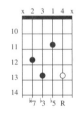 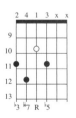 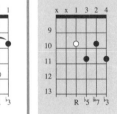 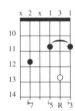 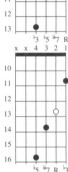

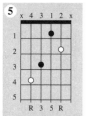

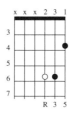

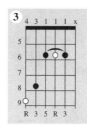

Maj
1, 3, 5

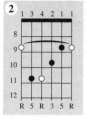
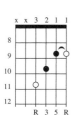

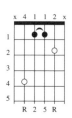
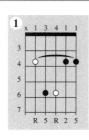

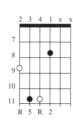
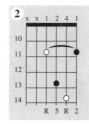

sus2
1, 2, 5

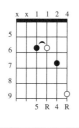

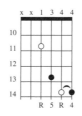

sus4
1, 4, 5

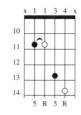

no 3rd
1, 5

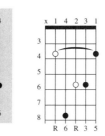

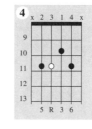
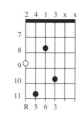

6
1, 3, 5, 6

D♭
C#

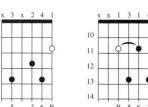

Maj7
1, 3, 5, 7

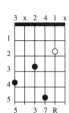

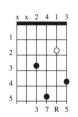

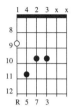

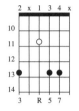

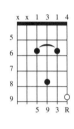

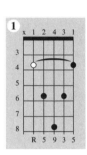

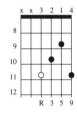

---

add9
1, 3, 5, 9

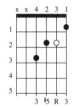

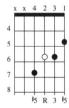

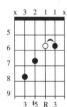

Augmented (aug)
1, 3, ♯5

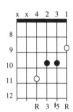

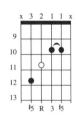

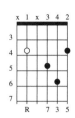

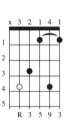

D♭
C♯

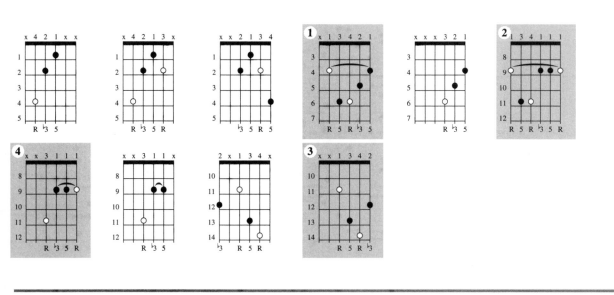
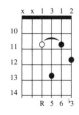

min
1, ♭3, 5

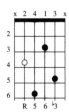   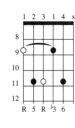

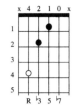 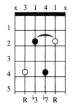   

min6
1, ♭3, 5, 6

 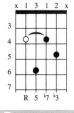  

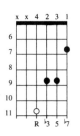   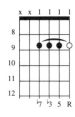

min7
1, ♭3, 5, ♭7

D♭
C♯

7

1, 3, 5, ♭7

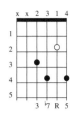 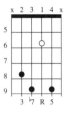 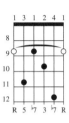  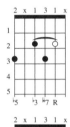 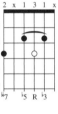 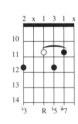 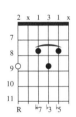

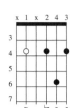   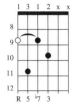  

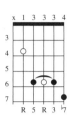 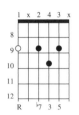  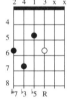 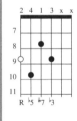

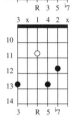 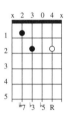 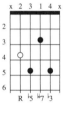 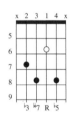 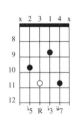 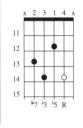

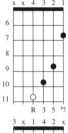 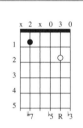  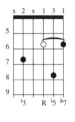 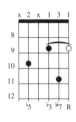  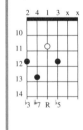

dim7(°7)

1, ♭3, ♭5, ♭♭7

  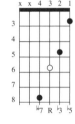 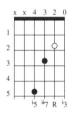 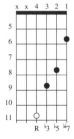 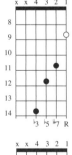 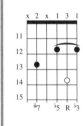 

D♭
C#

D

Maj
1, 3, 5

     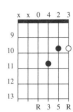

 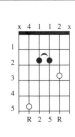 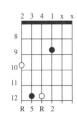  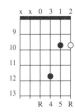 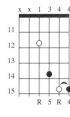

sus2
1, 2, 5

 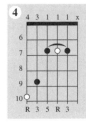 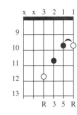 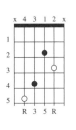 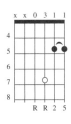 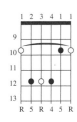

sus4
1, 4, 5

   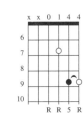  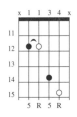

no 3rd
1,5

6
1, 3, 5, 6

  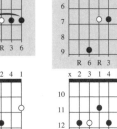   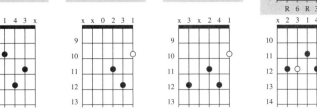

D

D

Maj7
1, 3, 5, 7

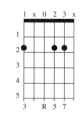 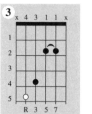 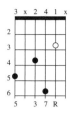 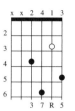 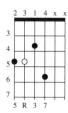

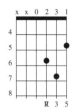  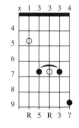 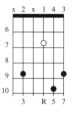 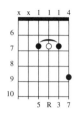

 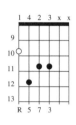  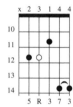 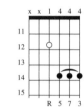 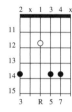

 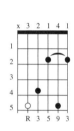 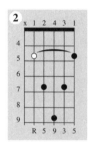 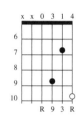 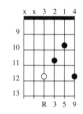 

add9
1, 3, 5, 9

  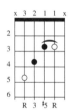 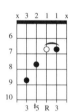

Augmented (aug)
1, 3, ♯5

  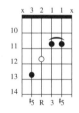

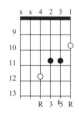 

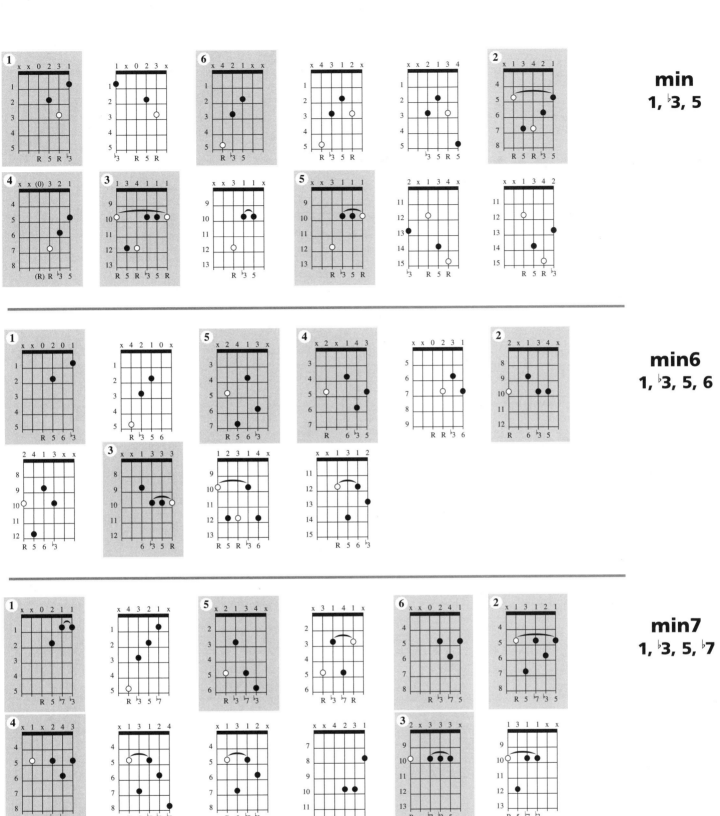

min
1, ♭3, 5

min6
1, ♭3, 5, 6

min7
1, ♭3, 5, ♭7

D

7
1, 3, 5, ♭7

dim7(°7)
1, ♭3, ♭5, ♭♭7

D

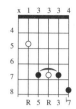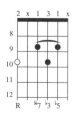
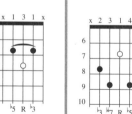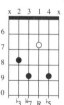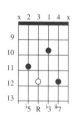
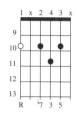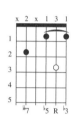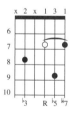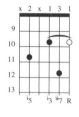
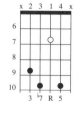
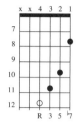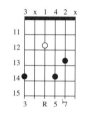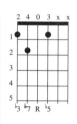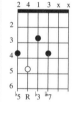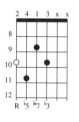
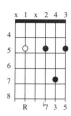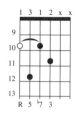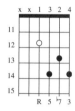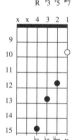

  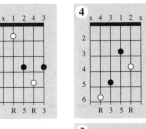 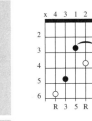  

Maj
1, 3, 5

   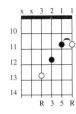

 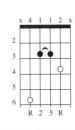  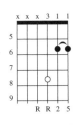 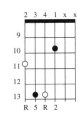

sus2
1, 2, 5

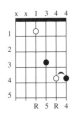  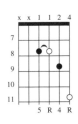  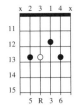

sus4
1, 4, 5

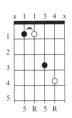  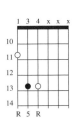

no 3rd
1, 5

  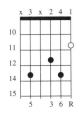  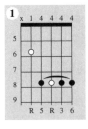 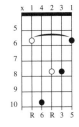 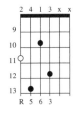

6
1, 3, 5, 6

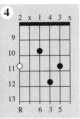

E♭
D#

Maj7
1, 3, 5, 7

 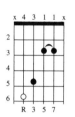  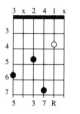 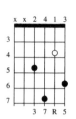 

   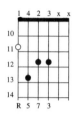 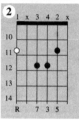

add9
1, 3, 5, 9

  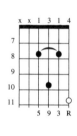  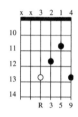

Augmented (aug)
1, 3, ♯5

  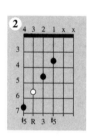 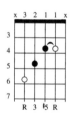

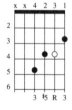 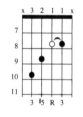 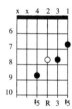 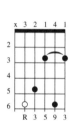

  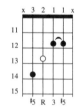 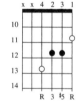

E♭
D♯

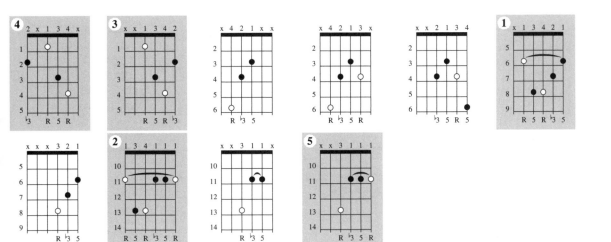

min
1, ♭3, 5

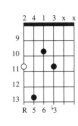

min6
1, ♭3, 5, 6

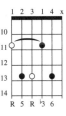

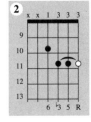

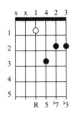
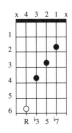

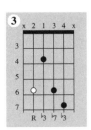

min7
1, ♭3, 5, ♭7

E♭
D♯

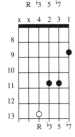

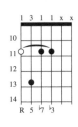

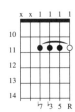

7
1, 3, 5, ♭7

   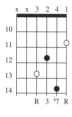 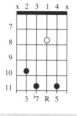  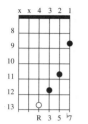  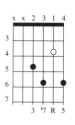 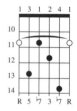 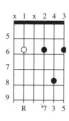 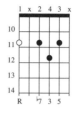 

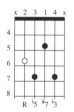 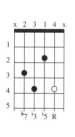 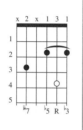  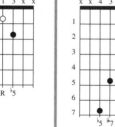

  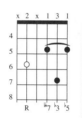   

dim7(°7)
1, ♭3, ♭5, ♭♭7

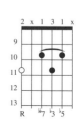 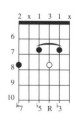 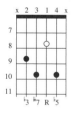 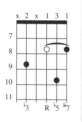  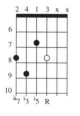 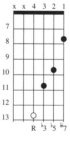

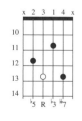 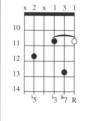 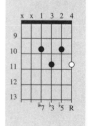 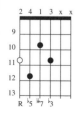 

E♭
D♯

E

Maj
1, 3, 5

    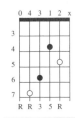 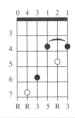

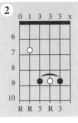 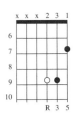 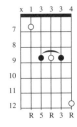   

sus2
1, 2, 5

  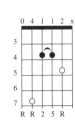   

sus4
1, 4, 5

 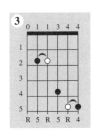 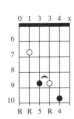 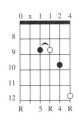 

no 3rd
1,5

 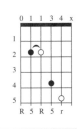  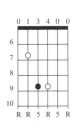 

6
1, 3, 5, 6

 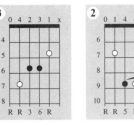   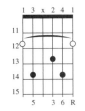

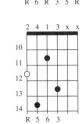 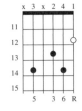

Maj7
1, 3, 5, 7

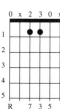
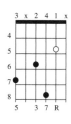
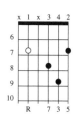
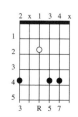
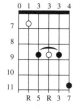

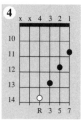

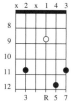

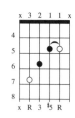

add9
1, 3, 5, 9

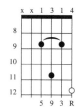
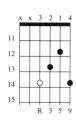

Augmented (aug)
1, 3, ♯5

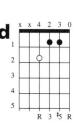
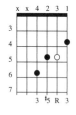

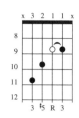
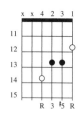
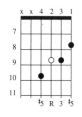

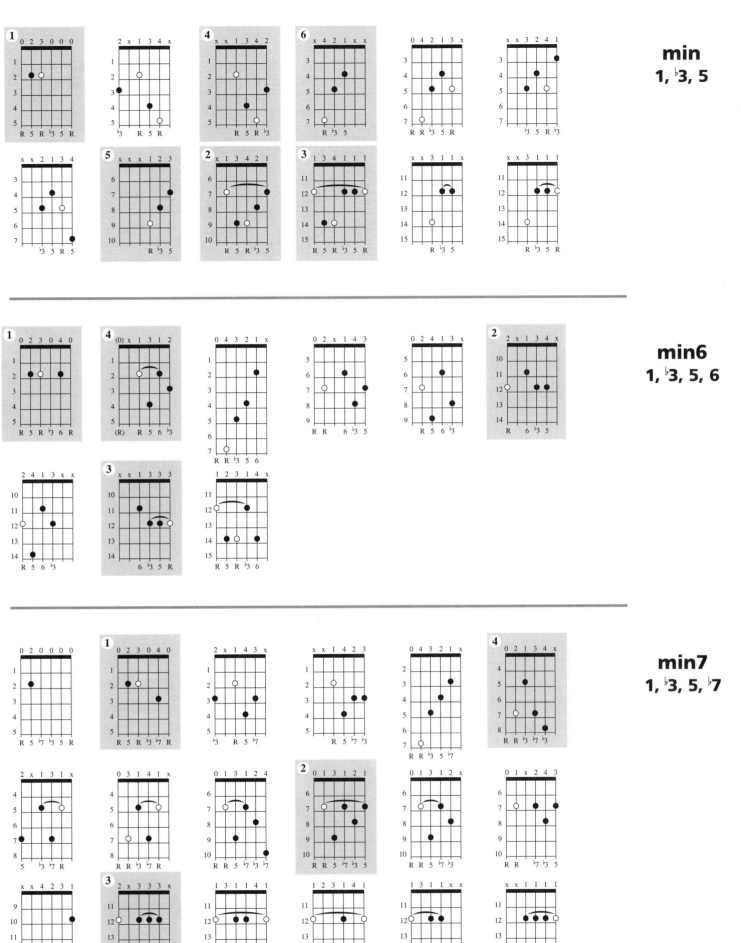

min
1, ♭3, 5

min6
1, ♭3, 5, 6

min7
1, ♭3, 5, ♭7

E

7
1, 3, 5, ♭7

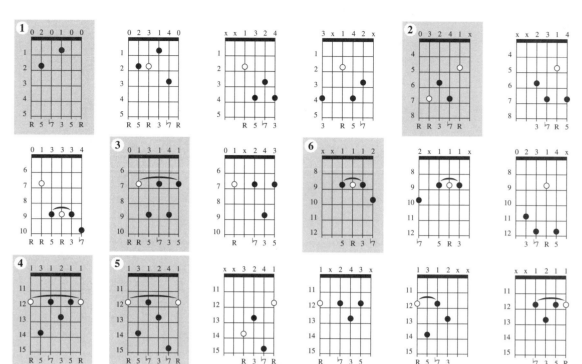

dim7(°7)
1, ♭3, ♭5, ♭♭7

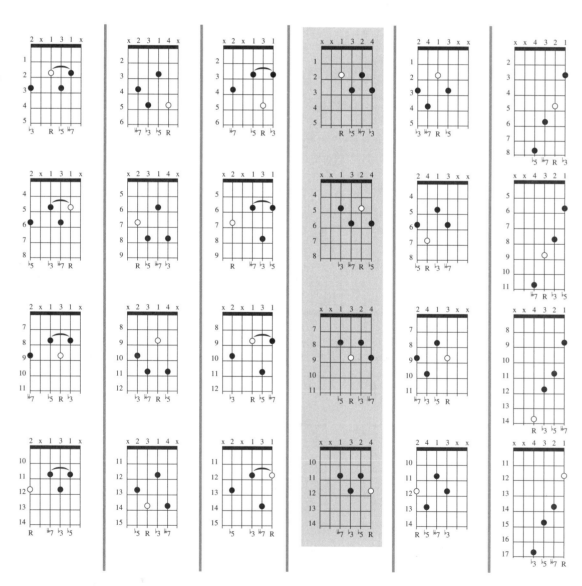

F

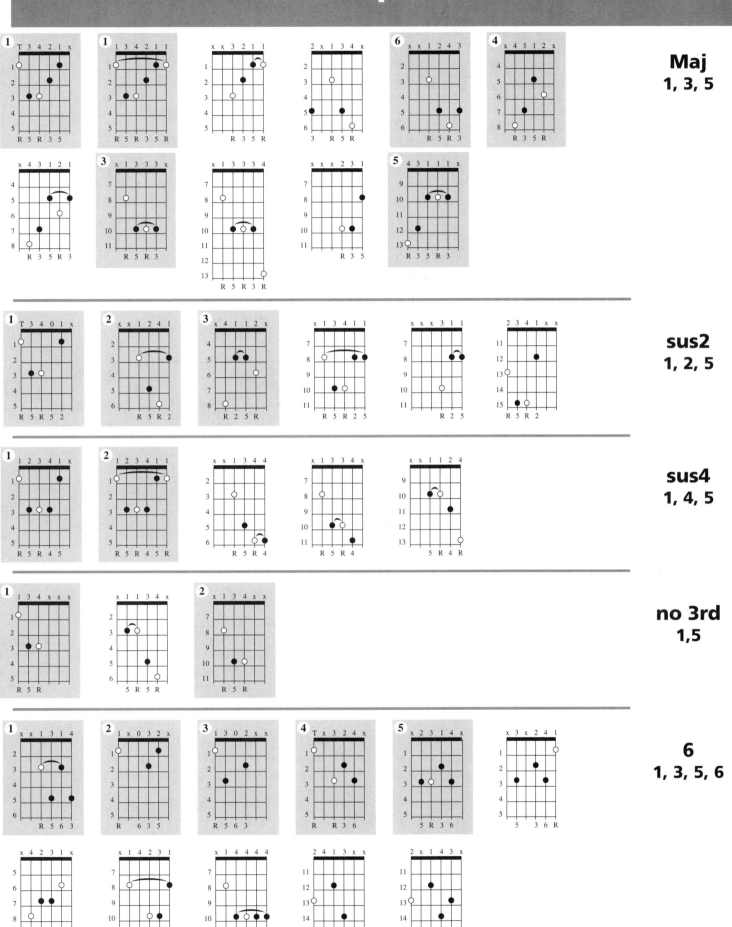

Maj
1, 3, 5

sus2
1, 2, 5

sus4
1, 4, 5

no 3rd
1,5

6
1, 3, 5, 6

Maj7
1, 3, 5, 7

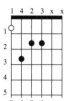  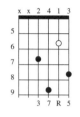  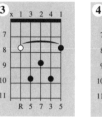  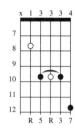

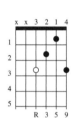 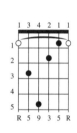   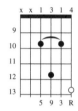

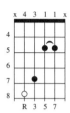 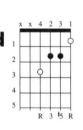 

F

add9
1, 3, 5, 9

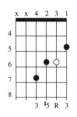 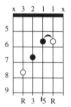  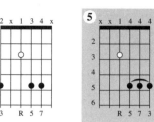

Augmented (aug)
1, 3, ♯5

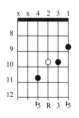 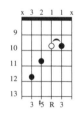 

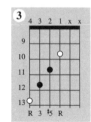

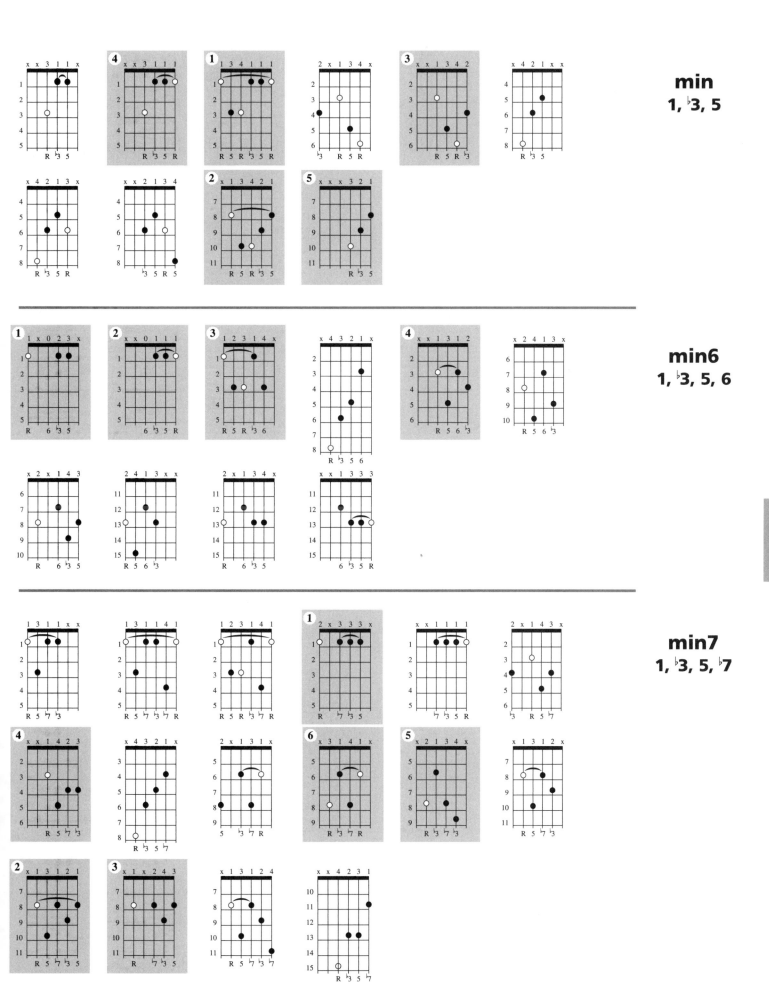

min
1, ♭3, 5

min6
1, ♭3, 5, 6

min7
1, ♭3, 5, ♭7

F

7
1, 3, 5, ♭7

dim7(°7)
1, ♭3, ♭5, ♭♭7

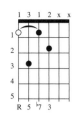  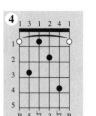 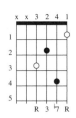 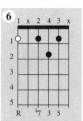 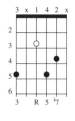
   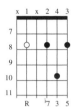  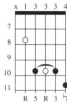
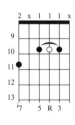 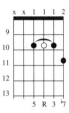 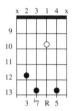 
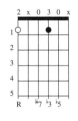 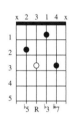    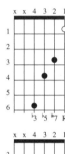
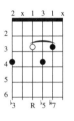 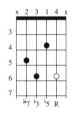 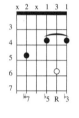 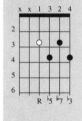  
 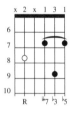   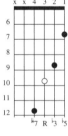
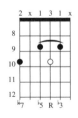 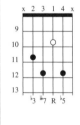 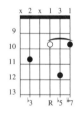 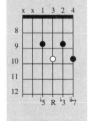 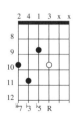 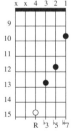
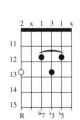 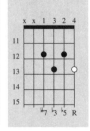 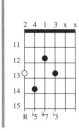

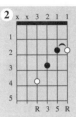

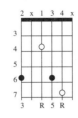
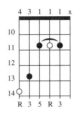
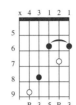

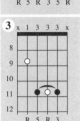
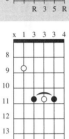
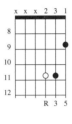

Maj
1, 3, 5

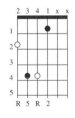

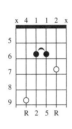
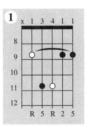
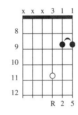

sus2
1, 2, 5

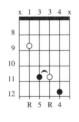
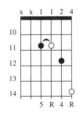

sus4
1, 4, 5

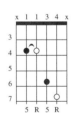
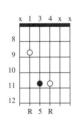

no 3rd
1,5

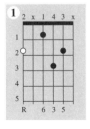
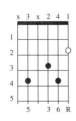

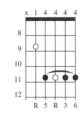

6
1, 3, 5, 6

G♭
F#

Maj7
1, 3, 5, 7

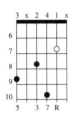  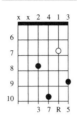 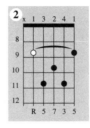 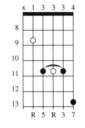 

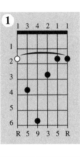 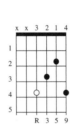 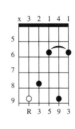  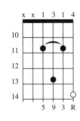

add9
1, 3, 5, 9

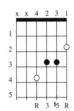  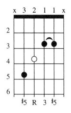 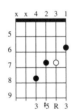 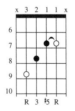

**Augmented
(aug)**
1, 3, ♯5

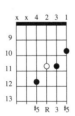  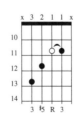

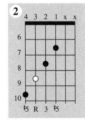

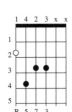    

G♭
F♯

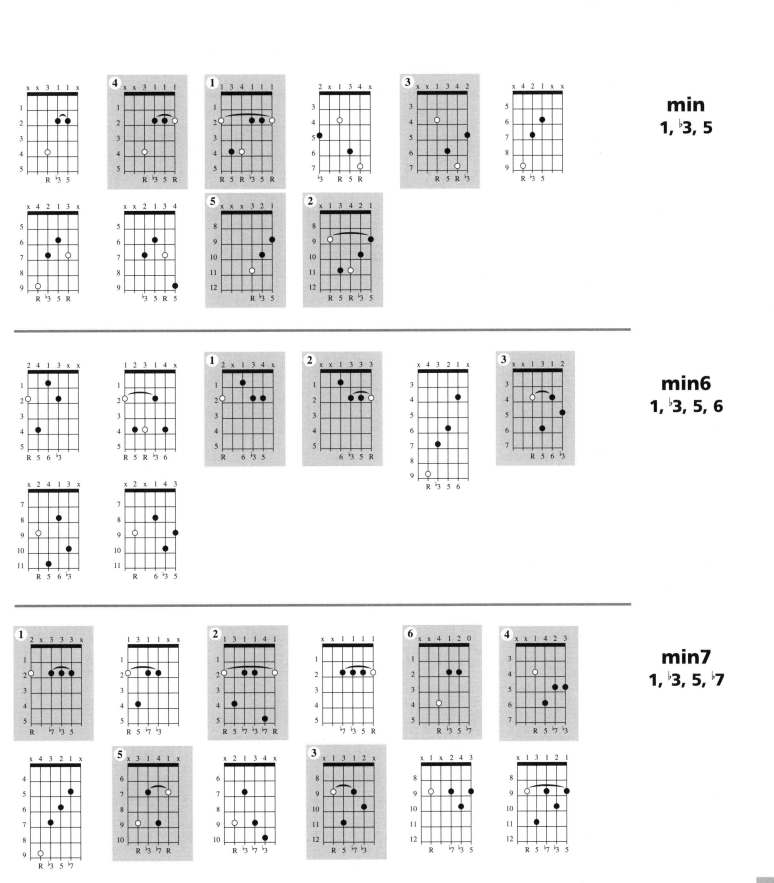

min
1, ♭3, 5

min6
1, ♭3, 5, 6

min7
1, ♭3, 5, ♭7

7
1, 3, 5, ♭7

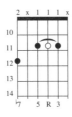 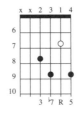 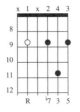 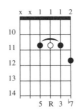 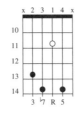

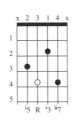

dim7(°7)
1, ♭3, ♭5, ♭♭7

 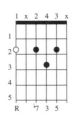 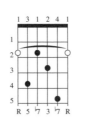 

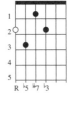 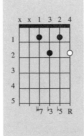 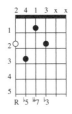 

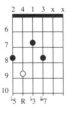  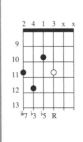 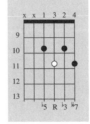

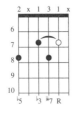 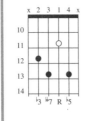 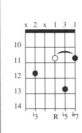  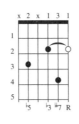

 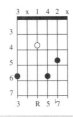 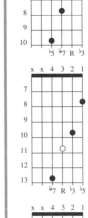

G♭
F#

G

 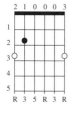 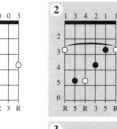 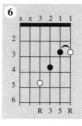 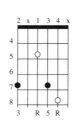 

  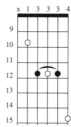 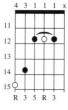 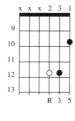 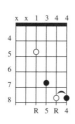

Maj
1, 3, 5

  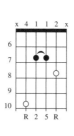 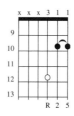  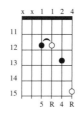

sus2
1, 2, 5

  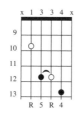  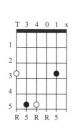

sus4
1, 4, 5

 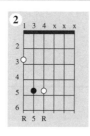 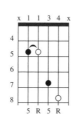 

no 3rd
1,5

 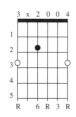 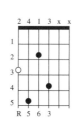  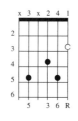 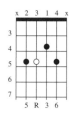

6
1, 3, 5, 6

* T = Thumb

    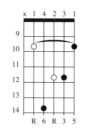

Maj7
1, 3, 5, 7

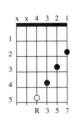

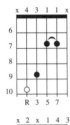
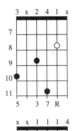
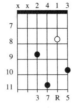

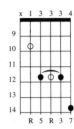

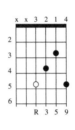
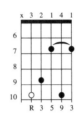
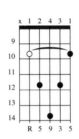
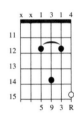

add9
1, 3, 5, 9

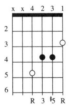

Augmented
(aug)
1, 3, ♯5

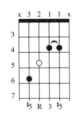
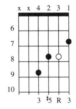

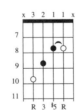
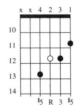

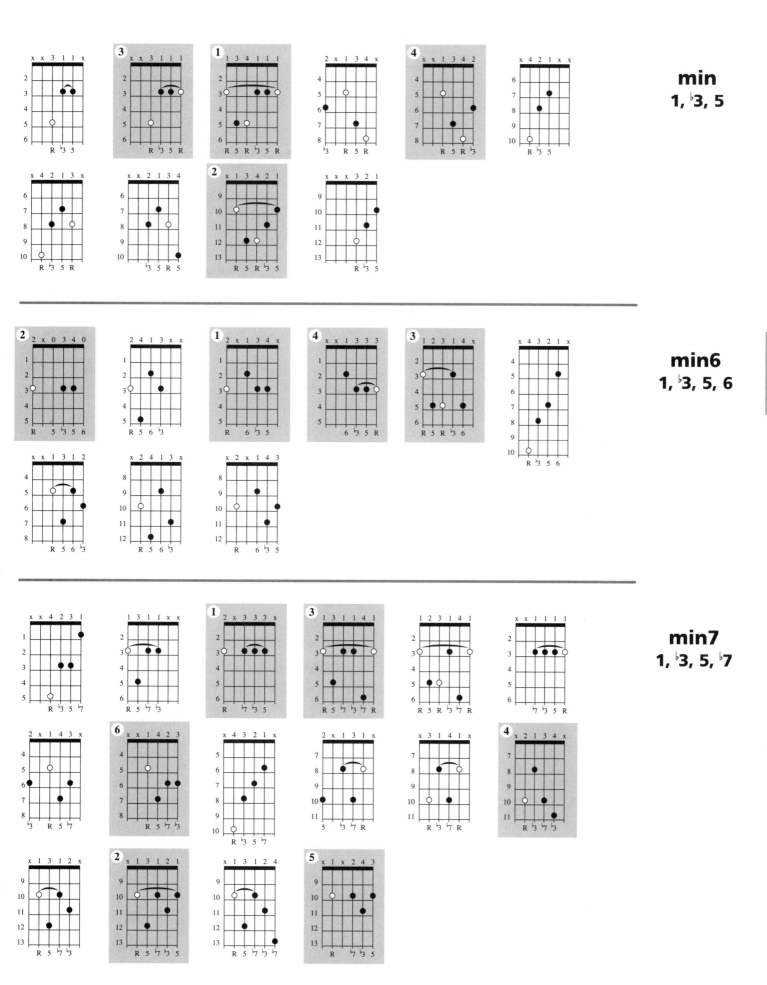

min
1, ♭3, 5

G

min6
1, ♭3, 5, 6

min7
1, ♭3, 5, ♭7

7
1, 3, 5, ♭7

  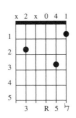   

 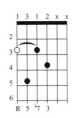  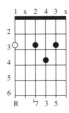  

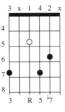   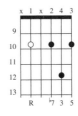 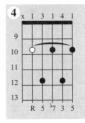 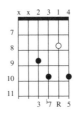

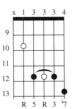  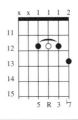 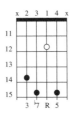 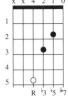 

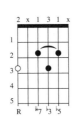 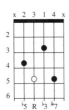    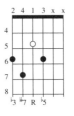

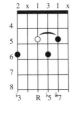  

dim7(°7)
1, ♭3, ♭5, ♭♭7

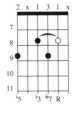 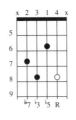 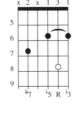  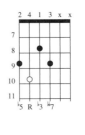 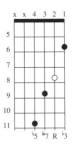

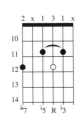 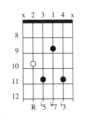 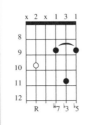 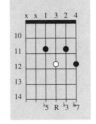 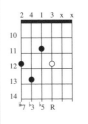 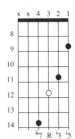

Guitar Fingerboard Chart
Frets 1–12

STRINGS

6th	5th	4th	3rd	2nd	1st
E	A	D	G	B	E

FRETS

Fret	6th	5th	4th	3rd	2nd	1st
Open	E	A	D	G	B	E
1st Fret	F	A#/B♭	D#/E♭	G#/A♭	C	F
2nd Fret	F#/G♭	B	E	A	C#/D♭	F#/G♭
3rd Fret	G	C	F	A#/B♭	D	G
4th Fret	G#/A♭	C#/D♭	F#/G♭	B	D#/E♭	G#/A♭
5th Fret	A	D	G	C	E	A
6th Fret	A#/B♭	D#/E♭	G#/A♭	C#/D♭	F	A#/B♭
7th Fret	B	E	A	D	F#/G♭	B
8th Fret	C	F	A#/B♭	D#/E♭	G	C
9th Fret	C#/D♭	F#/G♭	B	E	G#/A♭	C#/D♭
10th Fret	D	G	C	F	A	D
11th Fret	D#/E♭	G#/A♭	C#/D♭	F#/G♭	A#/B♭	D#/E♭
12th Fret	E	A	D	G	B	E

Fingerboard note markings

STRINGS: 6th 5th 4th 3rd 2nd 1st — E A D G B E

Fret	6th	5th	4th	3rd	2nd	1st
1st	F	A#/B♭	D#/E♭	G#/A♭	C	F
2nd	F#/G♭	B	E	A	C#/D♭	F#/G♭
3rd	G	C	F	A#/B♭	D	G
4th	G#/A♭	C#/D♭	F#/G♭	B	D#/E♭	G#/A♭
5th	A	D	G	C	E	A
6th	A#/B♭	D#/E♭	G#/A♭	C#/D♭	F	A#/B♭
7th	B	E	A	D	F#/G♭	B
8th	C	F	A#/B♭	D#/E♭	G	C
9th	C#/D♭	F#/G♭	B	E	G#/A♭	C#/D♭
10th	D	G	C	F	A	D
11th	D#/E♭	G#/A♭	C#/D♭	F#/G♭	A#/B♭	D#/E♭
12th	E	A	D	G	B	E

If you love this book,
you'll love our schools!

Online...

WORKSHOPLIVE

The next generation of music
education from the founders of the
National Guitar Workshop

**Take a FREE online
lesson today.**
workshoplive.com

...or Near You!

N · G · W

National Guitar
Workshop

LOCATIONS: Connecticut, Florida,
Seattle, Nashville, Los Angeles,
Texas, San Francisco, Virginia
...every summer!

1-800-234-6479
guitarworkshop.com